GOOD ✦ OLD ✦ DAYS®

RIDING THE
AIRWAVES™

EDITED BY KEN & JANICE TATE

Riding the Airwaves™

Editors: Ken and Janice Tate
Managing Editor: Barb Sprunger
Editorial Assistant: Sara Meyer
Copy Supervisor: Michelle Beck
Copy Editors: Mary O'Donnell, Läna Schurb

Publishing Services Director: Brenda Gallmeyer
Art Director: Brad Snow
Assistant Art Director: Nick Pierce
Production Artist Supervisor: Erin Augsburger
Production Artists: Nicole Gage, Janice Tate
Production Assistants: Marj Morgan, Judy Neuenschwander
Photography Supervisor: Tammy Christian
Photography: Matthew Owen
Photo Stylists: Tammy Liechty, Tammy Steiner

Printed in China
First Printing: 2010
Library of Congress Number: 2009928698
ISBN: 978-1-59217-270-2
1-59217-270-9

Good Old Days Customer Service: (800) 829-5865

RETAIL STORES: If you would like to carry this pattern book or any other DRG publications,
visit DRGwholesale.com

Every effort has been made to ensure that the instructions in this publication are complete and accurate.
We cannot, however, take responsibility for human error, typographical mistakes or variations in
individual work. Please visit AnniesCustomerCare.com to check for pattern updates.

We would like to thank the following for the art prints used in this book.
For fine-art prints and more information on the artists featured in *Riding the Airwaves* contact:
Applejack Art Partners, Manchester Center, VT 05255 (802) 362-3662, www.applejackart.com
Curtis Publishing, Indianapolis, IN 46202, (317) 633-2070, All rights reserved, www.curtispublishing.com
Norman Rockwell Family Trust, Antrim, NH 03440 (603) 588-3512

DRGbooks.com

1 2 3 4 5 6 7 8 9

Dear Friends of the Good Old Days,

"The airwaves belong to the people." That has been an oft-repeated phrase that was first hoisted as the United States Congress began debating the Radio Act of 1927.

I'm not here to start a political, social or constitutional debate as to whether or not "the airwaves belong to the people." But for the first generation of those of us who went riding the airwaves in the early days of broadcasting, I'll tell you that we *felt* like we owned the airwaves!

And in many ways, that made us feel like we owned the whole world.

After all, it was radio and television that brought the world into our homes. Before these amazing inventions gave us access to the airwaves, news of the outside world traveled slowly. In cities, the paperboys cried out "Extra! Extra!" as newspapers tried to keep up with the changing world. In rural areas, we were fortunate if a weekly paper made its way out to the farm.

Radio first—and later, television— were invited into our living rooms and became trusted friends. As our friends, radio and TV educated and informed us.

Broadcast journalist Walter Winchell greeted us: "Good evening, Mr. and Mrs. America … and all the ships at sea!" Edward R. Murrow, who added his voice during World War II, greeted us with, "*This* is London." He unflinchingly took us with him to the flames of London bombings and the horrors of the war front. He signed off each broadcast with the salutation that became popular in England during the *Luftwaffe* raids: "Good night, and good luck!"

The airwaves didn't just bring us information; they also brought us fun. No longer were the best acts restricted to city theaters and restricted by expensive tickets. We could hear the best comedians, the best vocalists, the best drama—the best everything—while we gathered around the radio.

By the late 1940s to the early 1950s, television wasn't just gaining a foothold; it was taking the nation by storm. Soon we saw our favorite personalities and programs—from *The Lone Ranger* to *Gunsmoke*, from Jack Benny to Red Skelton— make the jump to the small screen.

Soon we were watching the small, fuzzy screen to catch the World Series or *The Honeymooners* or *Dragnet* or *Captain Kangaroo*. We were captivated, mezmerized by the magic of television.

In 15 years of producing our *Good Old Days* books, my dear wife Janice and I realized we had never examined the phenomena of broadcasting and its wondrous effect on modern life.

These firsthand memories of radio and television, and how they changed our lives will take you back to the golden age of broadcasting.

So, whether or not the airwaves belong to the people, all of us felt like the world was a little closer and a little more real after we went riding the airwaves in the Good Old Days.

Ken Tate

⪻ Contents ⪼

Sitting 'Round the Philco • 6

The Time Machine in My House 8
Family Christmas Eve 11
That Ipana Smile.................................12
A Family Tradition................................15
Dusting the Philco.................................16
Tap Dancing on the Radio 18
The Magic Voice.................................22
Little Orphan Annie Secret Decoder Rings.........28
My Old Atwater Kent 30
Radio Man and Comics 33
The Witch's Tale.................................34
Theater of the Mind..............................36
Punishment?.....................................39
Cotton-Pickin' Radio 40

Programs That Changed Our Lives • 42

The Day Television Changed Our Lives 44
Radio Was King...................................47
Bride and Groom 48
A Wunnerful Afternoon 49
Of Mars and Men 50
Martian Invasion!.................................53
Princess for a Day 54
Lights! Action! 56
The Davis Sisters 58
A Beginning Never to Be Forgotten 60
Calling Captain Midnight 63

The Wonders of TV • 66

Early TV Times...................................68
Advice in Time 72
Our Admiral After-School Surprise 73
TV Favorites.....................................74

Lucy and Dish Night..77
Our First Television...78
The Impossible Scheme 82
Television Don 83
TV Was Young and So Was I 84
Not on My Roof 86
The Spelling Bee..87
Matches Lighting Up the Screen 88
The Big Event...89
Captain Video 90
Super Circus..91
For Better or Worse...92
Being First at Something....................................96
Shopping With Charlotte 99
The First TV Remote 100

Our Favorite Shows • 102

The Radio Rangers, Johnny Carson and Me.....104
Remembering the Pinkster 106
The Gum That Won the West...................................109
Turn the Radio On 110
Roy Acuff and the Grand Ole Opry............................116
Ding Dong School 120
The All-American Boy 122
Ma Perkins, Radio Adventuress 124
My Other Family, the Barbours 127
Radio's Most Popular Show 130

On the Air With ... • 132

Memories From a Golden Age..................................134
Me and the Captain 138
Good Morning, Captain! 141
Half a Century With Bergen and McCarthy 142
I Remember Olivio Santoro 146
Frank and Dr. I.Q. 148
Unforgettable "Noncelebrities" 149
Remembering Schnozzola 151
Art Carney 152
Happy Hopalong Daze 156
Freddie the Fireman...158

Sitting 'Round the Philco

Chapter One

For as long as I can remember, radio has had a magical hold on me. I can't explain it—but magic must be inexplicable in order to be magic, right?

I still like to go to sleep at night with a tape of *The Shadow* playing softly on the nightstand next to me. I often wonder if Mama put me to bed with the radio playing in the next room. Perhaps that's why the barely audible sound puts me to sleep so readily.

Radio had a way of breaking down the boundaries of distance and economics when I was a little boy. We were poor, but we could still listen to concert music all the way from Boston and New York. Dance music was live from Chicago. There were great comedies starring Jack Benny, Edgar Bergen and Charlie McCarthy, and Bud Abbott and Lou Costello. Action shows like *The Lone Ranger, Superman* and *Jack Armstrong—The All-American Boy* were enough to keep our hearts pounding.

Yes, radio was magical to me.

For me, the most magical broadcasts on the radio were the games of the St. Louis Cardinals. Harry Caray joined Dizzy Dean of the Gashouse Gang in the KMOX broadcast booth, bringing my father and me the play-by-play of our favorite baseball team.

Nothing cemented Daddy and me together more than the hours we spent listening to the Cardinals broadcasts, hanging on every pitch and cheering every run scored for the "good guys."

Jack Buck added his inimitable style to the broadcast booth in 1954. Our children listened to broadcasts by Harry and Jack, and later, Mike Shannon—and I think a little of radio's magic may have rubbed off on them as well.

I always wanted to take Daddy to a Cardinals game, but never got the chance. So he and I listened through the years as the old Sportsman's Park was renamed Busch Stadium, and then as the "new" Busch Stadium was dedicated in 1966. He died long before that one was torn down to make way for a new "new" Busch Stadium in 2005. But even in his old age, I joined him from time to time to listen to a game on a spring or summer evening.

As for me, I'd rather catch the radio play-by-play in my easy chair—Janice at my side catching up on some sewing—than watch the game on television. Magic is smothered when too much reality encroaches.

I still enjoy drinking in the ambiance and atmosphere on my radio. The stories in this chapter likewise capture the magic of the days when families gathered in their living rooms to catch the news, enjoy an evening of comedy and music, or just listen in as their favorite baseball team took the field.

Those were magical days and nights while we were sitting 'round the Philco back in the Good Old Days.

—Ken Tate

> *I still like to go to sleep at night with a tape of* **The Shadow** *playing softly on the nightstand next to me.*

The Time Machine in My House

By Ronald Scott

The radio sits today in a corner of my dining room, a large 1940 Philco console floor model with a warm brown veneer, designed in the smooth, curved, art deco style. A round, cloth-covered speaker, partially hidden behind vertical wooden strips, takes up the lower two-thirds of the space below a lighted horizontal station-selector dial with plastic knobs and ruby red push buttons.

I am older than this radio, but not by much. It's older than all of my brothers and sisters. As one of the first new items my parents purchased early in their marriage, the radio seemed a wonderful treasure among the hand-me-downs given to them when they set up housekeeping in Clairton, Pa., in the late 1930s.

This luxury cost about $40, not an inconsiderable sum at the end of the Great Depression. Still in its heyday in the 1930s and 1940s, radio dominated the airwaves through the middle 1950s until it was shouldered aside by television.

On this radio, I listened fanatically to the kids' popular after-school serials: *The Lone Ranger*, *Tom Mix*, *The Green Hornet*, *Dick Tracy* and *The Shadow*, "who, while traveling in the Orient, learned the secret to cloud men's minds so they could not see him." While I gobbled down Cheerios and other breakfast cereals that often sponsored these exciting radio adventures, I never could bring myself to drink Ovaltine, as much as I liked *Captain Midnight*.

Today, this large 1940 Philco console floor model sits in a corner of the author's dining room.

Comedy was important to lighten the harsh realities of life and hard work in those days, and it abounded on the airwaves. The whole family—mother, father, grandparents, myself, and later, my younger brother, Kenneth— gathered to listen to the countrified silliness of *Lum and Abner*, the clownish Red Skelton, the topical humor of Bob Hope, and the deprecating buffoonery of ethnic programs such as *Life with Luigi* and *Amos 'n' Andy*. An indifferent mindlessness pervaded the country then, and it would be years before a semblance of equality would protect immigrants and minorities from ridicule on the radio, in movies, on television, and eventually, in real life.

News came to us on this radio also, including the first shocking reports of the Japanese "sneak attack" on Pearl Harbor. Although too young to understand the significance then or what a war would entail, I learned quickly.

As I grew to school age, with a better understanding of events outside my town, I heard the voices of newsmen like Robert Trout and Edward R. Murrow, and the wonderful but frightening announcement of the D-Day Invasion on June 6, 1944, as General Dwight D. Eisenhower proclaimed the beginning of the "Great Crusade" to take back Europe from the Nazis. This was a fight in which my own father, by then, was engaged.

Less than a year later, I returned home one afternoon to find my mother huddled before the radio in tears. "President Roosevelt is dead," she said between sobs.

I cried because my mother was crying, but as a 6-year-old, I did not feel the real depth of her emotion. That would come some 18 years later when, on a different radio in another city, I heard the first flash reports from Dallas of the sudden loss of another president.

Over the years, the large Philco serenaded us with music, urged us to buy war bonds, and entertained us with famous actors and actresses re-enacting stellar movie roles on programs like *The Lux Radio Theatre*.

Whether we had seen the movies or not, we could hear Humphrey Bogart and Walter Huston in *The Treasure of the Sierra Madre*, Barbara Stanwyck and Edward G. Robinson in *Double Indemnity*, and Tallulah Bankhead and William Bendix in *Lifeboat*.

Sometimes a performer's exposure on radio was not always to his advantage. I remember my grandmother Bertha, a large, formidable woman who chain-smoked Chesterfields—

Office of Defense Transportation poster by Albert Dorne, 1945, House of White Birches nostalgia archives

probably displaying a generation gap in music appreciation—saying one afternoon during a performance of Big Band music, "I can't stand that singer's voice. I'd like to reach right into that radio, grab him and wring his skinny neck!" She was referring to none other than a young Frank Sinatra.

Sports programs filled hours in front of this radio too. Home baseball games were broadcast live from Forbes Field in Pittsburgh; away games were re-created in a KDKA studio by sports announcers reading Teletype messages sent from the site of the contest.

With my grandfather, we listened as Joe Louis beat Pittsburgh native Billy Conn for the heavyweight championship of the world.

Probably the best times spent around this big console radio, however, took place in the late 1940s and early 1950s, after my father returned from the war and an Army hospital. Two more brothers, James and Richard, had joined the family by then as part of the postwar baby boom.

After supper, darkness fell early on winter nights. Mother cleaned up the kitchen as we hurriedly finished our homework, and Father rested on the sofa after a day's work in the steel mill.

Some evenings we listened to the original radio version of *Dragnet* with Jack Webb, who eventually moved with his program to television, or *Gunsmoke*, starring William Conrad, who had the voice for Matt Dillon, but not the look, and didn't survive the show's transition to television.

On the most memorable evenings, we turned off the room lights and lay on the floor or sat in the soft glow made by the large radio dial as we tuned in the classic thriller programs

The author's parents, Althea and Frank Scott, in 1944, shortly before he went overseas to the European theater of combat. Pvt. Scott wears his Army uniform, and his wife wears a military-cut brown suit, typical of the 1940s, with her husband's Army insignia on her lapels.

of the day—*Lights Out, Suspense* and *The Inner Sanctum.*

The theater of the mind created anticipation and chills far better than early television or period movies could. Sitting in a darkened room, aided only by voices and sound effects, we were transported to the far reaches of the frozen Arctic or inside the tomb of King Tut. Perhaps the story put us in a lonely forest cabin, where a noise outside in the night might be a windblown branch, a hungry bear, or even the green ghoul who reportedly prowled the forest. And about this time, just when goose bumps formed on my skin, Father or one of my brothers would reach out of the dark to suddenly grasp the nape of my neck!

So the same radio is now mine. After rescuing it years ago from cobwebs and dust in my parents' basement, where it had long languished, I took it to my home in Pittsburgh. Then it came with me when I moved to Racine, Wis., where a repairman replaced the condenser and a vacuum tube. Eventually, I brought it to Houston, Texas, where an antique dealer supplied new plastic push buttons for the original Bakelite ones that had grown brittle and cracked with age.

We don't listen to the old Philco much nowadays. It still works, and its sound is deep and rich, albeit with a bit of static. Perhaps it needs an adjustment to the internal antenna coil. Who knows? Maybe, if tuned just right, that old radio—just like an old-time radio science-fiction drama—would prove to be a time machine, issuing forth those long-lost sounds and voices of my youth, of our youth as a family, and our nation's youth, as well. In a way, this radio *is* a time machine—a time machine of the mind. ❖

Family Christmas Eve

By Marcella Lange

Christmas Eve 1930 shall always play prominently in memories of my childhood in Los Angeles, Calif. The tree was small for that Depression-era Christmas; the bird was chicken, and the packages were few because "work was slow," as Papa said.

Nevertheless, the good-time feeling was in the air.

The front room, where our Philco sat, had been polished; the lace curtains washed, stretched and starched; the cushions plumped; the Axminster carpet swept down to the nubbin, the faint pattern of pink roses showing through here and there. The oak mantel with the curlicues that were such maddening dust catchers had been lovingly rubbed with oil so that the leaves and floral design of golden oak gleamed and glimmered around the mirror.

The newspapers and magazines were in a neat pile. Papa's leather Morris chair had been rubbed down, and the crack didn't even show. The Philco had been moved to one side of the Christmas tree, which took the place of honor in the corner.

Papa called us in to take our places. Then he turned off the lights, plugged in the tree lights and turned on the radio.

We *oohed* and *aahed* at the lights on our 25-cent tree. Then Papa said, "Now we'll hear *Myrt and Marge*, and then it will be time to open the packages. This may be the night."

We had been listening to *Myrt and Marge* each evening, Monday through Friday, for months. Everything stopped at our house when Papa tuned in the Philco and we heard the familiar melody. And we knew what he meant by "This may be the night." Oh, if only Myrt knew what we already knew!

The lights on our little tree burned brightly, and we heard the last half of a Christmas carol before the deep-voiced announcer came on and the music carried us into the backstage lives of Myrt and Marge.

It was Christmas Eve there too. How we hoped that tonight would be the night Myrt, the old Broadway hoofer, would discover that Marge, the poor kid she had befriended, was really her own daughter, her lost baby, grown up and sweet and dear to her heart.

One tree light burned out, and the whole set went (Papa had worried over those lights, but we couldn't afford new bulbs), so we sat in the dark. I was glad because no one could see the tears that slipped down my cheeks when Myrt found Marge. I heard a sniffle from my mother's corner, and someone else blew her nose.

I felt warm and happy inside. Here I was, sitting with my own dear family on Christmas Eve, the pine-tree smell mixed with the aroma of pie from the kitchen, and we were celebrating the birth of a Baby born so long ago. Now Myrt had found her baby too, and we were all together, and it was so wonderfully Christmas Eve in that magic, imaginative, radio-land time.

The haunting refrain of *Poor Butterfly* faded away and was quickly followed by *Jingle Bells*. Forever thereafter, *Jingle Bells* and *Poor Butterfly* have blended together for me when I think Christmas Eve. ❖

That Ipana Smile

By Lucy Tharp

I grew up on a farm in Cumberland County, Tenn., during the 1930s and 1940s. Jean was my older sister, but only by 18 months. Consequently, we were very close. We worked together, played together and spent much of our free time together listening to popular radio programs. But we were interested in more than just the radio programs. Jean and I really got wrapped up in some of the commercials. We would go around singing the Pepsi-Cola jingle:

> *Pepsi-Cola hits the spot,*
> *Twelve full ounces, that's a lot.*
> *Twice as much for a nickel too,*
> *Pepsi-Cola is the drink for you!*

You could actually buy a 12-ounce bottle of soda pop for 5 cents!

Then we started to get interested in some of the free offers from the radio sponsors. The *Lum and Abner Show* was sponsored by Horlicks Malted Milk Tablets. You could get a free sample box of the product simply by sending in your name and address on a penny postcard.

Jean and I ordered the free sample of Horlicks. About two weeks later, we received in the mail a small box containing 12 tablets. We thought they were delicious! When you dissolved one tablet in a glass of milk, you had instant malted milk! We stretched it out and made the box last about a week.

After that, we ordered a lot of free samples. Unfortunately, we ordered indiscriminately and received a lot of things we didn't need. Our greed and disdain for common sense was bound to get us into trouble. One of the Knoxville stations had a one-hour live program of country music that ran from noon until 1 p.m. Lots of different products were advertised on that program.

During one segment, a Dr. Vogue Larson would come on and make his spiel about a product he claimed to have invented in his own private laboratory. He called it "Vogue-Lar." Vogue-Lar, he said, was a "fertility tonic." He claimed to have helped thousands of women with fertility problems. "Send in your name and address to this station for a free sample," he said. "I know you will want to buy more."

We didn't know what *fertility* meant, but we had heard Dad talk about doing things to make our garden fertile. *If it's good for the garden, it must be great for girls.*

We ordered a sample. Fortunately, on the day the sample arrived, it was Mom who went to the mailbox. When she started to unwrap the small package, her face took on a puzzled expression. "What's Vogue-Lar?" she asked Dad, who was busy thumbing through a farm machinery catalog that had also come in the mail. Dad confessed that he was totally in the dark.

After reading some of the labeling, she immediately turned her attention to Jean and me. We tried to assume an air of innocence.

"Fertility tonic!" she exclaimed. "Did you order this stuff, Jean?" When Jean tried to avoid the question, Mom turned to me. "How about you? Did you order this?"

"We ordered it," I admitted. "We heard it on the radio, and we just wanted to see what it was. Dr. Larson said Vogue-Lar was good for women."

Mom gave us a stern lecture about being tempted to order items simply because they were free. "You never take *any* kind of medicine unless you know what you're taking it for!"

Dad took the Vogue-Lar outside and dumped it in the yard. When he came back inside he was shaking his head. "That stuff is nothing but legal moonshine," he said. "I'll bet it's at least 80 percent alcohol. It's a good thing I didn't pour it in the creek! It would make the fish drunk."

Mom finished her lecture with a firm warning: "You are not to order anything else off the radio without first getting permission from Dad or me. If anything else comes in the mail

that we didn't both OK, both of you are going to get a good tanning with the razor strop. Now you've been told. A word to the wise should be sufficient."

We adhered to Mom's caveat about sending for products advertised on the radio. But we rationalized that her warning did not extend to magazine offers.

A colorful advertisement in *Colliers* magazine caught our attention. It was an ad for Ipana toothpaste. Ipana was a popular brand of toothpaste back then. The ad showed a young, adoring couple beaming toothy, pearly smiles. "THE IPANA SMILE," the ad read. "KEEP YOUR *WHOLE* MOUTH WHOLESOME."

In our defense, it should be stressed that Jean and I were not as sophisticated and worldly as modern children are. We gave no thought to truth in advertising. If it was in a magazine or on the air, it must be true; otherwise, they couldn't print or say it, could they? And was there ever a girl who didn't want her whole mouth to be wholesome?

The ad offered a free sample of Ipana toothpaste. We remembered Mom's warning—and Jean reminded me.

"But that was *radio* offers," I replied. "This is out of a *magazine*."

Sis hesitated, then agreed. "I guess you're right. Maybe we could go ahead and order it. Mom probably won't care."

We didn't realize it at the time, but we were practicing what psychologists call "situational ethics." We were adapting our principles to fit a situation. We thought we needed the toothpaste, so it was all right to bend the rules.

But our decision to order the sample tube was a decision we were doomed to regret.

On the day the Ipana sample arrived in the mail, Mom and Dad had gone to town, leaving Jean and me at home.

It was a small sample indeed. The tube was about 2 inches long and as big around as a pencil. We wasted no time in getting some of that Ipana smile. By the time we finished brushing, there was only enough paste left in the tube for one more scrubbing.

Jean came up with what seemed like a great idea. "There's not enough for both of us," she said. "Why don't we brush Squash's teeth?"

Squash was our little mongrel dog. We called him Squash because he was the color of cooked squash. Squash seemed to take to the dentifrice like a fish to water. He seemed to enjoy the taste. The brushing also stimulated his salivary glands. He had worked up a nice froth around his mouth when we heard the sound of the family pulling into the driveway.

Now, Squash was a real daddy's dog. Whenever Dad returned home, even if he had been gone for only a few minutes, Squash insisted on running out to meet him.

But this time, as soon as Squash ran out of the house, we heard Mom let out a loud shriek. "Squash has gone mad! Look! He's foaming at the mouth!"

Jean and I walked out onto the front porch. Dad took one look at Squash and said, "That

dog's not mad. He's not sick. He's been eating something. It looks like soap."

Then Mom looked directly at us. "Did you girls do something to Squash?"

Her question was purely rhetorical. She knew we were guilty. There was nothing to do but confess. In Mom's court, there was no plea-bargaining and there were no appeals. We made a full confession to the whole sordid crime, hoping for mercy. But alas, no mercy was forthcoming.

"Remember my promise?" she said. "I told you if you ordered anything else without permission you would get a spanking. Now go up to your bedroom and wait. When I put the groceries away, I'll come upstairs to take care of business."

We felt like we were climbing the steps to the gallows. Mom rarely administered corporal punishment, but when she did, you were in for an unforgettable experience. But the pain was not the worst of it; *that* was over quickly. It was the humiliation.

We sat expectantly on the side of the bed, neither of us speaking. It was only a few minutes, but it seemed like hours before we heard Mom's footsteps on the stairs. Then she came into the room, the razor strop dangling from her hand.

"All right, let's get this little unpleasant chore over with," she said. "Lie down across the bed, facedown." I lay there, tensed up, waiting for the lick to fall. I heard the first whack and I thought, *Well, at least it doesn't hurt.* Then I realized the heat was falling on Jean.

We got 10 swats each. We tried to hold back our tears, but the blistering strop was too much. However, the crying, like the pain, didn't last long, and there were no grudges held by either party. By suppertime, we were back to our old, giggling, frivolous ways.

We did learn our lesson, though. We never again ordered merchandise without approval from higher authority. We learned the lesson of Proverbs 22:6: "Train up a child in the way he should go; and when he is old, he will not depart from it." ❖

> *"There's not enough for both of us,"* Jean said. *"Why don't we brush Squash's teeth?"*

A Family Tradition

By L. Wellington Miller

We would gather around it in the darkness, waiting in total silence as we stared, mesmerized, at the big, green, pulsating eye. Then it came to life. In 1943, I was 10 years old, the youngest of five children. We lived in the small town of Sunbury in northeastern Pennsylvania. My three brothers were in the military, fighting overseas, leaving only my sister and me at home.

Before the war, it had been a family tradition for all of us to sit around the radio and listen to the news and our favorite radio programs. Two of my father's favorites were *Hawaii Calls* and *The Kate Smith Hour*. *Hawaii Calls* was transmitted from so far away that the sound faded in and out like a shortwave radio broadcast.

Usually it was aired during suppertime on Sunday. That was the only day we had to be quiet at suppertime. Other days, we chatted and talked about our day. But that evening, it was different. It was a very special time for the whole family, but mostly for us kids.

Our tabletop radio was the old tube type, about 23 inches wide and 16 inches tall. When turned on, there wasn't instant sound as there is today. The tubes inside those old radios had to warm up before the sound would come on.

The lighted dial was on the lower right side of the radio. In the upper left corner was a 3-inch round eye of green glass with a small black pupil in the center. This was the indicator that let us know when all the tubes were warmed up. The black pupil became larger and larger until the green eye stopped pulsating. That meant the radio was ready for us to tune in our programs.

Majestic radio ad,
House of White Birches nostalgia archives

Two very long bare wires were connected to screws on the back of the radio. One was for the ground; my dad connected it to one of the steam radiators that provided heat for our house. The other wire was used as the aerial for reception. Dad ran that to the nearest window and let it hang outside.

We all had our favorite programs, of course. My brothers liked *Inner Sanctum* with the door that screeched as it closed. That was one of the scary programs. My sister liked the funny ones: *Fibber McGee and Molly*, *Jack Benny* and *Red Skelton*. My favorite was *The Lone Ranger*, which ran every Monday, Wednesday and Friday at 7:30 p.m. on station WOR in New York. He was my idol for years, and I often envisioned myself riding with him on the great horse, Silver.

But it didn't matter if our favorites weren't on. We just sat there and listened to whatever was on. *The Shadow*, *The Green Hornet* and *Death Valley Days* are among the many shows that I remember. The airways were filled with so many programs that we never became lonely.

For me, the amazing thing about the old radio programs was the fact they could transport me from our living room to wherever the story took me. Sitting in the dark, it was easy to fantasize and become part of the story the radio created.

Each night, my family gathered in front of that big, green, glowing eye and waited with anticipation. We listened to people with no faces, only voices. But those voices opened doors for us to wonderful places we would never really see. ❖

Dusting the Philco

By Jeannine Stone

In the mid-1940s, I was given the distasteful chore of dusting. I was 10. My job included gently wiping every curve and crevice on our 1940 Philco radio. I vividly remember sitting on the floor with a cloth hung over my pointer finger as I reluctantly stuck it between the slats that protected the speaker. I hated that job, and I claimed it made my finger sore. But Mother insisted it be done every Saturday. "No dust bunnies hiding in my house."

One day, after I finished dusting every difficult recess, I ran my soft cloth across the face of that Philco and saw something that intrigued me. On an oblong brown plastic plate were the names of cities that, at age 10, I knew little about. Hesitantly I turned the on-off knob and pushed one brown button after another. Eventually I found WGN Chicago. Mother scolded, "Jeannine, quit playing with the radio and see to your dusting."

There I was, in Kalamazoo, Mich., and I was listening to the other side of the world!

"But I found Chicago."

"Turn it off and get to work."

But when no one was around, I went back to the radio and twisted a couple of knobs and zeroed in on Central America. I noticed right away that the music was different from anything I was used to hearing. I tried to figure out if Central America was in Illinois or Iowa. At 10, I didn't know those things.

I turned another dial. Wow! After some static, I found music coming from across the ocean. I turned a knob and heard a voice speaking a foreign language. Was it Berlin, Paris or some other exotic place? I could hardly believe my ears. There I was, in Kalamazoo, Mich., and I was listening to the other side of the world! I was so excited that I had to tell someone about my find. I settled upon a neighbor.

Our neighbor Mr. Ellis had been born in England. He spoke with an interesting accent. I knew that he knew a lot of things about far-away places, so I knocked on his door. I asked him if he had a map that would show me what was on the other side of the ocean. He was pleased to tell me he did.

Mr. Ellis showed me a paper globe of the world, which he had made. I was so curious about how he had cut and glued a flat map into a sphere that I almost forgot what it was that I wanted to know. Finally I asked Mr. Ellis if I could look up Berlin, London and other cities that were listed on the overseas band on our radio. He helped me find them and told me which countries they were in.

Gathering Around the Radio by Ethel Pontsler © House of White Birches nostalgia archives

Of course, because he was from England, he told me many things about London and his homeland, including the fact that many of his friends and relatives were still there and having a tough time since World War II.

Next I asked if Illinois was in Central America. I was curious about the very different music that came from there. I was astounded to learn that Central America was not even in the United States! Mr. Ellis took my finger and ran it far down past the borders of Texas and California. He said, "You see, Jeannine, the reason the words and music from Central America are different from what you hear on our local radio stations, and even WGN Chicago, is because it is coming from a Spanish-speaking population."

"Is Spain in Central America?"

"No, Spain is in Europe. See? It's here."

And so went the conversation. When it was time for me to leave, Mr. Ellis gave me the paper globe with instructions to carry it carefully so it would not collapse. Who could have guessed that my dusting chore would turn into a geography lesson? Did Mother find out about it? Unless Mr. Ellis told, I doubt she ever did.

I think Mother would be surprised to know that in the late 1990s, I spent several years looking for a radio just like that Philco that I hated to dust. Today I own one, a fully restored 1940 Philco, which looks exactly like the one my parents owned. My husband bought it for me as a surprise from the Tulip City Antique Mall in Holland, Mich.

Now, dusting its fine curves and crevices never fails to bring back pleasant memories. Whenever I drape a dust cloth over my finger and stick it between the rungs that protect the radio's speakers, I can hear my 20-years-deceased mother saying, "Jeannine, turn off that radio and tend to your work."

I just smile as I dust, and enjoy music and voices from faraway places. ❖

Tap Dancing on the Radio

By Charlotte Anne Smith

I got a good laugh and a look of incredulity from my daughter when I mentioned that we used to listen to tap dancing on the radio. What is tap dancing but rhythmic sound? Apparently the casting directors of the radio variety shows shared that view, as tap dancers were frequently booked on the Bob Hope, Bing Crosby, Jack Benny and other variety shows, along with singers, comedians and even ventriloquists.

Yes, ventriloquists. After all, we couldn't see anyone's lips move—one of the advantages of radio. If we could have, Edgar Bergen might have had a lot more trouble becoming a star. By the time he got to television, we were all so hooked on the antics of Charlie McCarthy, Mortimer Snerd and Effie Klinker that we didn't care how much Bergen's lips flopped in the breeze.

We didn't need to see it to visualize what a mess the junk in Fibber McGee's closet made every time he ignored Molly's plea not to open the door—or how much money was in Jack Benny's vault each time the lock clicked and the door swung open.

Mommy was emphatic that Raymond Burr looked nothing like Perry Mason when the series moved to television.

It didn't matter at all what Dennis Day looked like. What counted was his high, clear notes as he sang the songs of Ireland on Benny's show.

Silver was just as white and the Lone Ranger's mask just as black when we listened to their adventures as they ever were after they moved to the silver screen.

Pat Buttram's little blue-nosed mule, Fleetwood, couldn't have brayed any clearer if it had been standing in our living room, and the landscape of Gene Autry's Melody Ranch looked just like it did in his movies. The coconut shells sounded just like real horses' hooves as Champion, Silver or Tom Mix's Tony chased down bad guys on the radio.

Giant goose bumps rose on our arms and the hair on our necks stood to attention every time the familiar creak sounded with the opening of the door to the *Inner Sanctum*. When that deep voice intoned "Who knows what evil lurks in the hearts of men—the Shadow knows," we didn't need to see his face.

When we moved to the country northeast of Fayetteville, Ark., when I was 4, there was no electricity there. The move meant we couldn't

Styled with Swagger...Packed with Power...Rarin' to Go!

PHILCO
Rough Rider
3-WAY PORTABLE RADIOS

Give and get the Luxury Look of Leather

You can't give finer—you can't buy better than a Philco "Rough Rider" Portable. Every beautiful and rugged model a *thoroughbred* . . . rarin' to go. Here's fashion leadership with an eye to roughing it. All the tough properties of the finest leather—unbeatable, unbreakable and, oh, so *portable!*

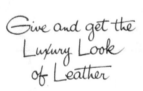

GENUINE TOP GRAIN COWHIDE

"Mustang" **3-WAY PORTABLE** — Leather-tough, leather-handsome! The real "powerhouse" of portable radios . . . all dressed up in rich Top Grain Cowhide. Case snaps open for easy change-over from AC-DC to batteries. Philco 676.

1956 Philco radio ad, House of White Birches nostalgia archives

enjoy the radio any longer, as the set we had wouldn't run on batteries. There was no more sitting in Daddy's lap and laughing with him at *Amos 'n' Andy* and the other comedy shows we had both enjoyed.

Then, in 1939, the REA line reached our place, and we had electricity once again. Daddy hooked up the old radio we had used in town, but the reception wasn't the greatest.

When World War II loomed on the horizon, Daddy bought a portable radio that was built for both electricity and batteries. It looked like

a small suitcase, complete with a handle on the top. To my knowledge, it never contained a battery, but it did bring in programs more clearly.

When the Miss Hush contest was running on Ralph Edwards' show, everybody in the neighborhood was listening to the clues and debating the identity of the mystery woman. There was a community Hobo Party at Sons Chapel the night Edwards' show was on, and after much pleading and a fair exercise of my dramatic ability, Mommy allowed me to take the radio to the party.

When it came time for the call to be made to the lucky person that was getting a chance to guess, everybody gathered around the radio, completely focused. That was the night someone guessed correctly that Clara Bow was Miss Hush.

While we could receive the signal from KVOO at night when it was operating as a clear-channel station, it came through very faintly at noon. That was when the most important program was on, *Johnny Lee Wills & His Boys*, broadcasting from Cain's Ballroom at 423 N. Main St. in Tulsa, Okla.

Sometimes in good weather I would take the radio outside and set it on the well curb, which was as far as the extension cord would reach. The reception was very faint, but Charley Horse, my candidate for successor to Trigger, would stand with his ear right against the radio until the program was over. Don't tell me horses don't know quality when they hear it.

Since we couldn't see the performers, and most of us didn't have the means to purchase magazines that showcased our favorite stars, each listener built up mental pictures of his or her favorites. Erle Stanley Gardner had never given a physical description of radio's Perry Mason, but Mommy was emphatic that Raymond Burr looked nothing like him when the series moved to television. I thought it was perfect casting, though; apparently my mental picture was much different from hers.

My Aunt Lo lived with us sometimes, and she was a devotee of soap operas. Each afternoon, as soon as I got home from school, I joined her in agonizing through the trials of *Stella Dallas*, *Just Plain Bill*, *Ma Perkins* and all the others that kept the airwaves hot. Mommy thought listening to soaps was the ultimate trash,

The author (right) and her brother Jim didn't restrict their imaginations to what they heard on the radio, as is evident from the getups they wore in this photo taken in 1938.

so the only time I ever heard them was when Aunt Lo was in residence.

As the news of the war in Europe became more and more threatening, Mommy became more conscientious about listening to the news each evening. In January 1941, the Arkansas National Guard was activated, and the field artillery units were sent to Fort Sill, Okla. On Dec. 7, 1941, a Sunday, we went to church at Oakland Baptist Church and then went home with the Danner family. We had planned to stay all afternoon and then return home after evening services. But at about the middle of the afternoon it started snowing, so at 4 o'clock, Mommy decided we had better head home. We had to travel about 8 miles over dirt and red clay roads to get there, and she didn't want to get stuck.

Right after we got home, she turned on the radio. Then we heard that the Japanese had attacked Pearl Harbor. For hours, she sat right by the radio while I walked the hall from living room to kitchen and back again with only one thought in my head: *Daddy was going to have to go to war.* I don't think supper ever crossed our minds.

He eventually did go to the African-European theater. The radio and newsreels at the movies provided us with the only glimpses of actual fighting that we ever saw or heard.

Nowadays we don't have to adjust to someone or something looking different than we had pictured it. Perry Mason looks the same to everybody, as they never had the chance to picture him any other way. Everything today comes with both audio and visual evidence. What a pity people will never have the chance to enjoy tap dancing on the radio like we did in the Good Old Days! ❖

The Magic Voice

By Michael Grogan

The first radio I ever saw resembled something put together from broken clocks and other pieces gathered from the city dump. In 1947, when I was 7, our family's talking box had its cabinet removed so that Dad could tinker with the radio's exposed guts. At that time, I lived in Mabelvale, Ark., and enjoyed listening to *The Lone Ranger* over Little Rock's ABC affiliate, KGHI. I always read *The Lone Ranger* comic strip in the *Arkansas Democrat*; that, coupled with the charisma of actor Brace Beemer, who played the masked man on radio, was my first taste of popular culture. *The Lone Ranger* was pure moralizing, but it was flavored with vigilantism, mystery and action that satisfied my hunger for adventure and wish for law and order.

I often had lunch with my Grandmother Crandall when she lived near the railroad tracks. She churned her own butter and made ice cream from grape Kool-Aid, milk and sugar. She often baked jelly rolls with crimson jelly she had put up the previous summer.

> *Radio was reassuring.*
> *Like clockwork every evening at 6,*
> *Morgan Beatty read the news.*

After lunch, I usually played in the driveway next to the open dining room window. Here the radio soap operas drifted outside where I was skylarking about. The stories were mainly concerned with scandalous women who had dared to get a divorce. Divorced women were exciting—their activities set tongues wagging. And children in their late teens were always causing grief for their soap-opera relatives.

Ma Perkins had a heavy burden. For 15 minutes every weekday, she agonized over every heartache and nagged at her children, who seemed to take delight in defying her advice. Nothing much happened each day; soap-opera plots moved at a snail's pace, and the Oxydol soap commercials consumed six minutes of every scheduled quarter-hour of misery and despair.

At noon each day, Bob Wills and his Texas Playboys dished up good western swing music. My lifelong affinity for country-and-western melodies was formed then. The sad love songs almost reduced me to tears!

When my father entered the Methodist ministry in 1948, I had to leave dearest Mabelvale. Then, in 1951, my father became the pastor of the Dalark Circuit, a charge of four rural churches. Many Friday afternoons, our 1947 Plymouth coupe pulled up at Grandfather's

house, and we raided the cookie jar. I was glad to return to Mabelvale.

Radio was reassuring. Like clockwork every evening at 6, Morgan Beatty read the national and international news events. After the news, the soaper, *One Man's Family*, aired for 15 minutes over NBC. The program was sponsored by Miles Laboratories, makers of Alka-Seltzer, One-A-Day vitamins and something called Miles Nervine, which sounded like a remedy for schizophrenia.

After supper at Gram's house, we kids played until dark. I didn't get to listen to adult radio very often though. Grandfather Crandall listened to *The Fat Man*, a detective thriller, in his small living room. Golden light spilled down the rest of the darkened house as my brother and I slipped beneath the cool, sweet-smelling sheets of the roll-away beds in the semidarkness of the storage room. The radio's drone echoed like disembodied spirits.

Each Monday was a fresh slate. Sometimes after school in the early fall afternoons, the waning light of day had a golden-orange glow. Our little handful of chums put fresh red paper rolls of caps in our Texan Jr. cap pistols. We chewed Fleer's Dubble Bubble gum and shared boyish jests. We drew strength from our togetherness and fired our cap pistols like frontier marksmen.

Mutual Network's *Tom Mix* Western detective serial aired at 5:45 p.m. Monday through Friday, though by 1950, the show was winding down its long run. Curley Bradley played Mix, and the drama was set in the rural environs of Dobie, Texas. Sheriff Mike Shaw always pronounced Mix's first name like it was "Tome." (It is a testimonial to cowboy great Tom Mix's endurance that his radio show lasted a decade after his untimely death in a 1940 car wreck.)

Mark Trail was an afternoon adventure program based on the outdoor character created by cartoonist Ed Dodd. This show gave dubious advice; one episode explained that the force of a dynamite blast is less dangerous at the point of detonation, being more lethal on the periphery.

On Saturday mornings, I sat down near the exposed innards of our radio and listened to *No School Today* starring Big Jon and Sparkie. Sparkie was an imaginary boy with a tinny-sounding voice made by playing a recording at the wrong speed. Big Jon was the only adult on the program. Sparkie belonged to a secret club whose leader was called "the High Exalted Llama of the Purple and White Order." Mayor Plumpfront, Renfro Hencrow and Hogarty Fogarty were some of Sparkie's chums.

On today's television, the half-hour of music and song has vanished. In 1940s radio, you could hear the voice of Kate Smith, "The Songbird of the South"; Bing Crosby's romantic crooning drifted over the airwaves like the scent of honeysuckle blossoms; tenor Morton Downey Sr. had a voice that flowed like a stream; and Eddy Arnold, "The Tennessee Plowboy," sang, "I'm sending you a big bouquet of roses, one for every time you broke my heart!" As television comedian George Gobel used to say, "You cain't hardly get that kind any more!" (At least not on radio!)

> *In 1940s radio, you could hear the voice of Kate Smith, "The Songbird of the South" ...*

The radio comedies were truly funny. *Fibber McGee and Molly* starred Jim and Marian Jordan; this was a weekly visit to 79 Wistful Vista. Teeny (the little next-door girl), the Old-Timer, Wallace Wimple (who was henpecked by his wife, Sweetie Face), Doc Gamble and Mayor LaTrivia all dropped by to match wits and sarcasm with McGee. There is a touch of humorist James Thurber about Fibber; he is baffled by modern technology. And McGee's hall closet was a hazardous vicinity. For various reasons, somebody always opened the chamber of horrors, and a cascade of boxes, broken furniture, sporting equipment and secondhand appliances clattered to the floor with the sound effects of a landslide.

The Great Gildersleeve starred Hal Peary and, later, Willard Waterman. Gildy's full name was Throckmorton Philharmonic Gildersleeve; he was the water commissioner of Summerfield. His niece was Marjorie; his nephew was Leroy (played by shrill-voiced Walter Tetley). Birdie, the black maid, was the conscience of the family circle, and her dire predictions of calamity were usually correct.

Let the modern reader think that the male radio character was unaware of seductive women, but a drawling Southern belle named Leila Ransom caused Gildy's heart to flutter. Her deep Southern vernacular was one of radio's most erotic feminine voices!

Jack Benny's radio show on Sunday nights (circa 1951) had a simple premise. Each week Benny had conferences with his regular cast about what he would do on his next week's radio show. Benny's radio character loved money almost as much as life itself. His legendary basement full of money was guarded by a man who reputedly had not seen the outside world in decades!

Naive Dennis Day sang Irish songs after sharing dialogue with Benny and his cast. Mary Livingston, Jack's real-life spouse, was Benny's loyal girl Friday on radio who knew she would never

The beloved comedian Jack Benny smiles from the NBC microphone in this publicity photo from the 1940s. Photo courtesy House of White Birches nostalgia archives.

see a penny of Jack's money. The only way skinflint Jack would marry her was if Mary came with a sizable dowry. Mel Blanc (voice of Warner Bros. Cartoon characters) was the sound of Jack Benny's eccentric mode of transportation, a 1919 Maxwell. And who could forget Eddie Anderson who played Rochester van Jones, Jack's valet?

The *Chase and Sanborn Hour*, sponsored by the famous coffee company, starred a ventriloquist named Edgar Bergen. Charlie McCarthy was another playboy whose sly sexual innuendos managed to elude the censors. Wooden dummy McCarthy wore a monocle, top hat and a dark formal suit. He liked booze, high living and dames. Charlie could dish out insults to guest stars in the manner of Don Rickles. Mortimer Snerd, a country bumpkin, was so stupid that he actually made sense in a fractured sort of way. He was also a wooden dummy. W.C. Fields often guested on the Bergen show, calling Charlie McCarthy a woodpecker's snack bar. Field's distaste for the dummy was real!

On Saturday night at 8:30, the National Broadcasting Corporation aired a half-hour segment live from WSM Nashville, Tennessee's *Grand Ole Opry* direct from the old Ryman Auditorium. The Opry was an institution dating back to 1925, and it featured the nation's best pickers and grinners. Comedians Rod Brasfield and Minnie Pearl kept the audience in an uproar with their cornball jokes and tart comments. Somber Roy Acuff and smooth Red Foley alternated as hosts. The Old Hickory Singers with Claude Sharp provided barbershop harmony. The show had no formal script; the performers just penciled in their basic routines and winged it. The half-hour was sponsored by Prince Albert Smoking Tobacco.

Singing cowboy Gene Autry had a half-hour show each Sunday night. Just before his program began, there was a pause, and then a few notes on a guitar sounded on the coast-to-coast network before Gene sang his theme, *Back in the Saddle Again*. Autry sang beautiful Western ballads along with current favorites. He traded cornfield humor with comic Pat Buttram, who called Gene "Mr. Artery." The younger audience enjoyed the 10-minute Western drama starring Gene, Buttram and Johnny Bond. In the early 1950s, Gene Autry was a hero to millions.

When I tuned to the *Green Hornet* radio program, I always felt like running for a flyswatter. The theme was a bridge lifted from the classical composition *Flight of the Bumblebee*. Britt Reid, the "real identity" of the Green Hornet, was a distant kin to the Lone Ranger, and he was the bane of evildoers.

The Lone Ranger and *The Green Hornet* were both produced by George W. Trendle. The Hornet's faithful chauffeur, Kato, was much like the Lone Ranger's Tonto. Kato drove the Black Beauty, a custom-built speedwagon.

The Hornet used a tranquilizing gun that put villains to sleep for a half-hour. Reid worked on *The Daily Sentinel* and his fellow reporter, Michael Axford, thought the Hornet was a meddling vigilante who should be put out of business. Lenore Case was the Green Hornet's female heartthrob, but because this was a juvenile show, they couldn't display overt sensuality.

The 1945 radio series called *The Sealed Book* had an intro that said that there were many stories in the Sealed Book, and each episode came from this cosmic diary. In one story, some thugs convince a woman that they are ghosts. When the thieves go outside to complete their scam, the woman locks them out of the house. The temperature drops quickly, and it begins to sleet and snow. The crooks come to the front door and beg to be let in, as they are freezing to death. The woman believes they are ghosts even through the men try to dissuade her from thinking so. The next day, they are found frozen to death on the front porch— victims of their own scheme!

The airwaves were thick with private detectives. *Nick Carter, Master Detective*, was loosely based on the pulp hero who was good with disguises. *Barry Craig* starred William Gargan, and when Craig got hit on the head, he went "Hoop!" Many 1950s detective programs were influenced by the Mike Hammer novels of Mickey Spillane, which were big then.

The FBI in Peace and War and *Gang Busters* were an English professor's nightmare. The crooks used crude slang; there were bursts of gunfire, sirens, the roar of high-powered sedans and the blood-curdling yells of the female lead. The background music for such shows featured abrasive horns. There was little cultural value in these shows, which were just cheap, perishable, violent playlets.

The Shadow was a gothic mystery that aired each Sunday afternoon. Lamont Cranston possessed the hypnotic ability to cloud men's minds. As the Shadow, he brought dangerous criminals to justice. His girlfriend, Margo Lane, was his mistress, but the depth of their romantic entanglement was only a rumor. The plots revolved around the usual supernatural trappings: werewolves, mad scientists, ancient curses, haunted houses and the like.

Tobacco companies were prominent advertisers on radio. Each night at dusk, shows like *The Chesterfield Supper Club* featured singer Perry Como. Another cigarette advertiser bankrolled the *Camel Caravan*.

At night, it was delicious fun to go fishing down the AM band. I could hear a lovely hula girl singing on *Hawaii Calls*. The crash of the booming surf, the sound of steel guitars—then we waited for host Webley Edwards to speak in his dreamy tones. I could hear somebody being murdered as another episode of *Mr. Keen, Tracer of Lost Persons* was getting underway. A musical medley babbled in the background as I roamed the broadcast band.

Now, more than 40 years later, I feel sad for that wishful boy in Dalark. He has aged, and radio as it once existed is dead and buried. It wasn't that radio was so captivating—it was the only magic voice we had! The nation had weathered perilous times; radio made us laugh while war raged in Europe. Radio placated our fears; it informed us.

That era is gone, but I just feel thankful that I got to hear the great popular heroes and legends of our times. I feel like one of a dwindling band of pioneers who have actually heard old-time radio live in 1951.

"This is the end of our broadcast day. Here is our national anthem, *The Star-Spangled Banner*. Goodnight!" ❖

Little Orphan Annie Secret Decoder Rings

By Harris Akell

During the late 1930s and early 1940s, every afternoon at 4:30 you could hear this blaring from every radio in the neighborhood: *"Who's that little chatterbox? / The one with pretty auburn locks? / Whom do you see? / It's Little Orphan Annie!"* This theme song was always introduced by the announcer, Pierre Andre.

Like most grammar-school kids my age, I sat in front of a cathedral-shaped radio in the parlor, staring at the speakers so as not to miss a word of that day's exciting adventure. Before television, radio was the main source of entertainment for families. Adults had their programs, but we kids owned the late afternoon with adventure programs such as *Little Orphan Annie*.

At the end of every broadcast, Pierre would instruct all club members to take out their decoder rings and listen for the secret message. The only way you could decode it was by using the official Little Orphan Annie Decoder Ring.

Pierre Andre would start: "Number 4, B7, A9 … ." At this point, I felt that I was missing the most important part because I didn't have the decoder ring. I wanted one more than anything else, even more than the famous Red Ryder BB gun. But in order to get the ring and the official membership card, I had to send a label from a jar of Ovaltine with 25 cents to the address given by Pierre.

> *In order to get the ring and the official membership card, I had to send a label from a jar of Ovaltine with 25 cents.*

This was not a simple matter because I couldn't stand the taste of Ovaltine. My mother had bought me a jar once, and I had refused to drink the awful-tasting malt-flavored stuff.

Now, when I asked my mother to buy a jar, she said, "Absolutely not. You didn't like the taste when I bought it for you before, and besides, money doesn't grow on trees." The last part about the money was a standard statement given by most parents.

But I was tired of feeling left out, so I made up my mind that somehow I was going to find a label. At least that way I wouldn't have to drink that awful-tasting stuff that could ruin a good glass of milk. I would have to make a safari through neighboring backyard trash barrels in search of an empty jar with its label intact.

Facing page: 1936, 1937, 1938 and 1939 Radio Orphan Annie
Secret Society decoder rings, House of White Birches nostalgia archives

I lived in a neighborhood of three-decker houses built close together. Most of the families were headed by blue-collar workers who worked in defense plants. World War II was on. Food and gasoline were rationed.

The kids in the neighborhood frequently rummaged through trash barrels for usable items. A discarded roller skate or baby-carriage wheel—a rare find—coupled with two 2 x 4's and a wooden crate could be used to make a wagon.

A broken broomstick was used for stickball, and empty pop bottles could be redeemed for 5 cents each at the grocery store. We used the money to pay the 25-cent admission to the Saturday matinee. We didn't realize then that this was the beginning of what today we call "recycling."

In a backyard two streets away, I found an empty Ovaltine jar with the label intact. I couldn't believe my luck. Who would be so foolish as to throw out something so valuable?

I rushed home and carefully tore the label from the jar so the treasure wouldn't be damaged. I put the label and 25 cents from my allowance in an envelope and sent them to the address I had heard so many times.

After three agonizing weeks, the package bearing my decoder ring and official membership card finally arrived.

That afternoon, I could barely wait for the program to begin. Today's adventure was of no interest to me. All I could think about was the secret message. I was finally

going to find out what these secret messages were.

Finally, the adventure ended. Pierre Andre told everyone to take out their rings, and he announced the letters for that day's secret message: "A4, A6, B2 … "

I copied the code, letter by letter, onto a piece of paper so that I wouldn't miss any of them. When the last letter was announced, I took my ring in hand and started to decode my very first message as an official club member. This was exciting! The seemingly jumbled letters actually spelled a sentence.

My hands shook with excitement. When I was through deciphering the message, I stopped to read it.

As I read the message, I felt that I must have missed something, so I decoded the message again. But it read the same: "Drink your Ovaltine to grow big and strong and tune in to Little Orphan Annie's adventures every day at this same time."

How disappointing! After all the anxiety of waiting for the decoder ring and deciphering a message that was not as secret as I thought, I was disappointed and angry. At that moment I decided that I did not want to grow big and strong, at least not with the help of Ovaltine. In my eyes, *Little Orphan Annie* had cheated me, taking hard-earned money from a little kid.

With the wisdom of an 8-year-old, I mumbled, "With a message like that, no wonder Annie is an orphan!" ❖

My Old Atwater Kent

By R.C. Tuttle

Our first radio was a crystal set built by my father. It was simply a coil of thin copper wire wound around a round oatmeal box, with a crystal, a connecting wire and earphones. By connecting to a long, outside aerial, we could trap the radio waves in the coil and feed the signal through the crystal into the earphones. The year was 1925, and we lived about 30 miles north of New York City in a small town overlooking Long Island Sound. I was 9 years old and completely fascinated by this magic oatmeal box that could pull music and speech out of thin air without batteries or any form of electric power.

In time, improved homemade sets with tubes and batteries, built by some of the local "Roaring '20s Edisons," began to appear in the neighborhood. One creative World War I veteran wound his coils on discarded toilet-paper rolls.

> *It was filled with tubes and mysterious wiring, and it had state-of-the-art controls.*

One day my father came home with a brand-new Atwater Kent radio. It was filled with tubes and mysterious wiring, and it had state-of-the-art controls for volume and stations.

At that time the broadcast stations were WJZ, WABC, WOR, WINS, WEAF and a local station, WFAS. Our long outdoor aerial could pull in all of them, easily beating out the toilet-paper sets. Each night would find my mother relaxing in her easy chair, knitting; my father reading the paper; and me, stretched out on the floor, doing my homework—a portion of our brains intent upon the output of the speaker. Hey! I could do arithmetic problems while helping a radio detective in a whodunit! Our Atwater Kent quickly became the fourth member of our family, entertaining us day and night.

We usually started our evenings with *Amos 'n' Andy*, Lowell Thomas and the news, and *Captain Tim*. Captain Tim, a British stamp expert, discussed stamp collecting for 15 minutes. He was very popular with my father, an avid stamp collector.

In the mornings, there was an exercise program featuring a piano player named Bill who accompanied the announcer as he rattled off the exercises. We never did the exercises, but it was fun listening to the exerciser's comments. Occasionally he would have Bill play a piano solo, and Bill would always play the old standard, *Bye Bye Blues*. My father, a good piano player, used to play along with Bill. I was learning the piano at the time, and thanks to Bill, *Bye Bye Blues* was the very first popular song I learned.

Also in the mornings, there was the news, read as it arrived at the studio, unedited and unspun. During the day, of course, my mother had her choice of soap operas.

Two early programs we enjoyed were *Tomkins Corners* and *Main Street*, both similar in that they reflected life in a small town. There were many funny characters in both. *Main Street* had a town brass band that sounded like a herd of stampeding elephants. An occasional episode would include band practice—musical chaos. One had to hear it to appreciate the din.

Another program, *Joe and Vi*, was based on a comic strip and featured the theme song *Mean to Me*. Joe was the idiot husband who had a knack for getting into difficult situations before finally being rescued by Vi. Another program featured Frank Crumit and Julia Sanderson. Frank

played the guitar, Julia sang and both engaged in pleasant chatter. My father and Julia were kids together in Springfield, Mass., and the two used to be in school musical programs together. You can bet that that program was required listening.

On Sunday nights, we visited Doctor Watson and had a cup of G. Washington instant coffee with him as we listened to a Sherlock Holmes mystery. We also heard Rudy Vallee, Paul Whiteman, mystery and horror programs—and let's not forget the football games. During the 1920s and early '30s, Notre Dame dominated the football scene, and how we cheered when Army finally beat them! We also listened to the Dempsey-Tunney fight with the long count and yelled insults at the referee.

Another day, in 1927, we were thrilled to hear an excited announcer break into a program to tell us: "Lindbergh has landed in Paris!" We heard speeches by Calvin Coolidge, New York's Al Smith and other public figures.

Another program worth mentioning was *Duffy's Tavern*, "where the elite meet to eat. Duffy ain't here. Archie the manager speaking." Duffy was *never* there.

The Atwater Kent played on, needing only a new tube now and then. As the years went by, we bought other radios. My mother had one in the kitchen, my father had his car radio, and I had a small set in my bedroom. New programs came and went like the tide. However, the old Atwater Kent still owned the living room. Jack Benny, Bob Hope and other performers entertained us via the old set as did many musical programs and sitcoms.

When the Big Band era arrived, the Atwater Kent seemed to enjoy filling the room with music by Glenn Miller, Tommy Dorsey, Benny Goodman and the others. It was still going strong when I left for college in 1936.

On Dec. 7, 1941, I was home for a visit, listening to one of the Big Bands, when a voice abruptly broke into the music: "Our naval base at Pearl Harbor has been attacked, and our fleet has been destroyed!" Several months later, I was in the Navy, headed for the South Pacific war zone.

After the war, I came back home and saw that there was a new radio in the front room. The old Atwater Kent had been retired to the cellar. I went down to the cellar and found the set in a dusty corner. I set it on a table, plugged it in and turned it on. I was greeted by silence, so I looked inside the case. Wires, resistors, condenser and coils were literally fused together. It would never speak again.

Goodbye, old friend. You gave us countless hours of pleasure and kept us informed through the years.

I took the set home with me and gave it to a man who collected old radios. As far as I know, it still sits on a shelf in his shop, silently contemplating the strange world of transistors, TV, computers, lasers and other scientific wonders. ❖

Radio Man and Comics

By Kathy Trower

That Sunday morning in November 1949 was just one more cold, wintry day in our small Pennsylvania community. The wind howled through the bare trees, and the chimneys puffed white clouds of smoke. I recall fondly the cozy warmth of our neighbor's kitchen in direct contrast to the bitter cold I had experienced while walking to her house.

In that kitchen, at 9 a.m., three youngsters were gathered: my next-door neighbor, a city boy who was visiting his grandmother, and me. Before us, laid across the table, were the Sunday comics. The radio crackled as the deep voice boomed, "Welcome to *Sunday Morning Comics*." Then the voice read the funnies depicting the antics of Dagwood and Mr. Dithers while our eyes followed the pictures.

The sound effects—horses, the howling wind, crying babies—all came to life as "the radio man," as we tenderly called him, read the brightly colored newspaper panels.

This was a Sunday-morning ritual for Michael, Eleanor and me. Michael lived in the city and visited his grandmother, Mrs. Gavert, on weekends. Eleanor and I lived near each other and talked all week about Michael coming to his grandmother's house.

On Sunday morning, when Eleanor called my name at the fence, I would run out so that we could take the short walk to Mrs. Gavert's house. Sometimes we braved snow and rain to complete our journey.

By the time we took off our snowsuits and boots, we were exhausted from carrying the extra weight of heavy, wet clothes.

Then Michael, Eleanor and I would gather around the comics at his grandmother's kitchen table. The coal stove warmed the room and a cup of cocoa warmed our cold bodies. The aroma of coffee, which we were too young to drink, permeated the cozy room.

After the radio man finished his reading 30 minutes later, Eleanor and I would return home.

Years have gone by. And yet, when I read the comics today, I can still hear the *clip-clop* of the horses and the cry of the baby—and yes, I can smell the cocoa that warmed us on those Sunday mornings.

I lost touch with Eleanor when I married and we moved out of state. By coincidence, my first job was with a large company in the city where

1946 Sentinel radio ad, House of White Birches nostalgia archives

Michael lived, and I was elated to find that his mother was one of my co-workers. She and I visited many times during my tenure there, and we talked about the radio man and the comics.

She said that Michael would not miss a weekend at his grandmother's because he, too, enjoyed this ritual.

Today the comics are not so much in vogue as they were in those days. I often wonder if the comic-strip artists and the radio man knew how much enjoyment they gave three little children on blustery Sunday mornings.

Those days are gone, but the memories will always be there. ❖

The Witch's Tale

By Doris M. Kneppel

"Draw closer to the fire. … Stare into the embers and listen while Shadow—'*M-reow-w*!'—and I tell you 'The Tale of the Bloody Queen'!" Her evil voice sent shivers down my spine. I knew it was a dark, moonless night because I could see her as I stared at the radio. She sat cross-legged before a small fire in the middle of an empty field. In the light of the fire I could see her black shrouded figure, but her eyes were hidden in the shadow of her tall, pointed hat. Her long nose and pointed chin were caught in the light of the fire, and in the flickering shadows, I could see her evil black cat, Shadow.

Although I couldn't see the witch's eyes, I knew she could see me! She beckoned me with a long, gnarled, pointed finger. Shadow sat tall and straight next to her and stared into the fire. His eyes were cruel green slits, but they glowed in the light of the flames. His low, snarling yowl punctuated each of the witch's commands.

Such was the power of radio that our imaginations were always working overtime.

The flames licked upward, forming strange shapes—a foreboding of terrible things to come! Tonight the flames formed a castle surrounded by a moat. As I stared into the embers, swirls of mist crept up, and the walls of a gray castle emerged from the mist.

The scene was set. Soon I would "see" this evil queen, no doubt covered in blood. Had she stabbed someone? Was that why she was called "the Bloody Queen"? Or was she covered with her own blood? As I sat in the dark, staring at the radio while these thoughts swirled, I was deliciously frightened by the shadows cast by the radio dial on the walls of my room. The radio commercial did not interrupt my thoughts because the witch's querulous voice had set the scene, and my imagination was fleshing out the setting.

It was 1934, and I was a 10-year-old with an imagination developed by listening to radio stories and reading books. It is difficult for today's 10-year-old to appreciate the power that radio had to stir the imagination. The image of that witch is as vivid in my mind's eye today as it was more than 50 years ago. I would have been devastated if I had seen ordinary people reading a script and making the sound effects. Part of me knew the witch was not real, but another part of me accepted her as real in form and substance.

My dearest friend, Olivia, never got to hear this radio program because it was on past her bedtime. But being best friends carried with it the responsibility of remembering every detail of each story so that I could retell it in complete detail as we walked to school the next morning. It was fun to imitate the witch and Shadow, and use all the voices as I retold every detail with all the drama I could muster. And Olivia was a perfect audience. She squealed and shivered in all the right places. She often begged for another recounting (which, of course, I was delighted to provide).

Olivia would play at my house after school, and when dusk came, she would beg me to walk her home. Her home was on the other side of a cemetery. In daylight, Olivia and I were brave, but at dusk, our overactive imaginations informed us that the cemetery was a threatening place. After all, many of the witch's tales were set in a cemetery!

Olivia and I were not afraid of any person who might be lying in wait behind a grave marker. In those days, we occasionally came across a hobo curled up behind a tombstone, seeking shelter from the wind. But these unfortunates were too tired, too drunk or too hungry to pay attention to a couple of 10-year-olds.

No, we were terrified that a dead person would leap out from behind a tombstone or reach a skeleton hand out of the earth and grab our ankles! Such was the power of radio that our imaginations were always working overtime.

Since I was the older by three whole months, I appointed myself Olivia's protector. With great bravado, I accompanied her through the cemetery if it was close to dusk. I allowed Olivia to beg a story, and drawing from my repertoire of *Witch's Tales*, I would retell one.

The setting was perfect, and we were brave and giggly in each other's company. However, by the time Olivia waved goodbye and disappeared into her building, dusk had

turned to dark, and I had to go back through the cemetery alone!

The combination of having scared ourselves with spooky radio stories and being alone in the dark cemetery was enough to make me take a deep breath and race through the graveyard at top speed. I was always grateful when I made it home without having met the Bloody Queen or the Creeping Hand!

While I was a teacher, my students often asked how I managed without television when I was a child. They found it difficult to believe

Vintage postcard, House of White Birches nostalgia archives

that radio dramas could be more fascinating than television, for the same reason that we often complain that movie versions do not do justice to the original books. No one's interpretation of the written or spoken word can match our own imagination. We carry with us our own private picture of what we consider to be beautiful or fearful. The horror that we conjure up is far more frightening than anyone else's interpretation on a television or even a movie screen!

Radio provided my generation with a rich fantasy life. Now radio dramatizations are a thing of the past. But the same excitement and thrill awaits us whenever someone tells a story around a campfire, or when we read a well-written book! ❖

Theater of the Mind

By Sam Ewing

Young-at-heart old-timers remember the 1930s and '40s, when we enjoyed movies on radio: action with John Wayne in the classic Western, *Stagecoach*; William Powell and Myrna Loy in *The Thin Man*; Gary Cooper's *Mr. Deeds Goes to Town* and dozens more. They were big, big movies with big, big movie stars. The "theater of the mind" put us in a comfortable front-row seat at home. And yes, we actually sat and stared at Atwater Kent radios as if moving pictures were appearing on the set. In those days, it was exciting entertainment.

The four major network shows that specialized in putting movies on radio were *Hollywood Hotel*, *The Lux Radio Theatre*, *Screen Guild Theater* and *Screen Director's Playhouse*.

Hollywood Hotel, inspired and driven by popular, powerful and feared gossip columnist Louella Parsons, was the first major movie program to originate in the motion-picture capital. The mammoth one-hour production premiered on CBS on Oct. 5, 1934, and ran until 1938.

Warner Brothers singing star Dick Powell was the original master of ceremonies. Later he was replaced by a series of hosts—William Powell, Fred MacMurray and Herbert Marshall.

Movies dramatized on *Hollywood Hotel* included *Of Human Bondage* with Margaret Sullavan, *Death Takes a Holiday* with Gale Page, and the *Hollywood Hotel* feature movie, based on the program itself, starring crooner Powell.

The giant *Lux Radio Theatre*, one of broadcasting's all-time great attractions, also burst onto the national airwaves

Clark Gable was one of the many big stars featured in radio movies.

in October 1934. It was originally a Sunday-afternoon show, but soon moved into its long-running Monday-at-9 slot, where it commanded a huge weekly audience of 40 million—a third of the United States' population.

Superstars competed for a shot on *Lux Radio Theatre*. The show drew them like flies to honey. Cary Grant appeared 22 times, Barbara Stanwyck, 23, and Claudette Colbert, 24.

The major stars were paid a flat fee of $5,000. Clark Gable insisted on getting $5,001 just to be able to say that he, the king of MGM and filmdom, was also the highest-priced star on radio. Run-of-the-mill weekly productions used two big names; special shows boasted three or four. Production costs were the highest in broadcasting.

The Lux soap people understood that you get what you pay for, and they estimated that the stars' on-air endorsement of their product would be worth the price. They were right. Housewives flocked to stores to buy Lux. It became America's best seller.

Master filmmaker Cecil B. DeMille, maker of such epics as *King of Kings* and *The Ten Commandments*, hosted the program in its early years.

As emcee, DeMille earned $2,000 for each appearance. The super showman would have gone on forever under this financial arrangement, but fate in the form of the American Federation of Radio Artists (AFRA) stepped in. AFRA assessed members a dollar each in a campaign to strengthen union control in broadcasting. DeMille violently opposed paying the $1 as a matter of principle. A court battle ensued, pushed by DeMille, to the United States Supreme Court. He lost. Beginning with the 1945 program season, he either had to pay a dollar to AFRA or get out of radio. He got out.

DeMille's exit brought a series of guest hosts—Lionel Barrymore, Walter Huston and others—until William Keighley (a DeMille soundalike) was announced on November 1945 as permanent master of ceremonies.

Screen Guild Theater was first heard in 1939. In all of radio, no show succeeded in wooing more top stars than this one. And the stars generously donated their fees to the Motion Picture Relief Fund (MPRF). More than

Above: Shirley Temple is pictured with Johnny Russell in her classic movie, The Blue Bird *(Fox, 1940). A month before the film premiered, Shirley reprised her role on radio's* Screen Guild Theater, *donating her acting fees to the Motion Picture Relief Fund. Below: Actor Cary Grant, pictured in a publicity photo for his film* North by Northwest, *was a popular figure on the radio airwaves. Photos courtesy House of White Birches nostalgia archives.*

$800,000 in star fees was paid into the charity fund in just one season.

Immediately after turning down $35,000 for a single radio appearance by child-star Shirley Temple, her parents allowed the moppet to go on *Screen Guild Theater* on Christmas Eve 1939 in a radio adaptation of her film *The Blue Bird*. Shirley was paid nothing. It went to the MPRF.

Every star in Tinseltown was anxious to appear without payment on *Screen Guild Theater*. When a star dropped out because of illness or some other reason, producers were swamped with offers to take his or her place.

The *Screen Director's Playhouse* was a Hollywood extravaganza following closely in the footsteps of the *Screen Guild Theater*, with the added element of participation by renowned directors. Directors of the year's best films appeared and reminisced briefly about making their movies. Some of the classics heard on this popular program were *Fort Apache*, featuring John Wayne and director John Ford; *Jezebel* with Bette Davis and director William Wyler; and *Call Northside 777* with James Stewart and director Henry Hathaway.

Since those "movies on radio" were broadcast live, flubs were prevalent. Veteran screen stars suffered mike fright. Joan Crawford's hands shook so much she couldn't hold her script for her role in *Chained*. The pages had to be placed on a music stand and turned by an attendant.

Others admitted their terror. Just the thought of broadcasting to so many millions terrified big-name stars like Ronald Colman, Gary Cooper and Grace Moore. Paul Muni was so unnerved that he once played a violin right up to airtime to work out the tension.

There were lots of close calls. *The Plainsman* was a near-disaster. Co-stars Gary Cooper and Jean Arthur both suffered attacks of the flu at the 11th hour. Frederic March was called in to replace Cooper, but he had to take a crash course in diction to handle the Western dialect, which was foreign to him.

Actors goofed frequently and referred to their fellow performers on the air by their real names instead of the character names the scripts called for. We heard one performer called "Bing," another, "Ronnie" and a third, "Bogie," for Crosby, Reagan and Bogart. One famous actor, forgetting he was on live radio coast-to-coast, misread his line and burst into a string of expletives that shocked America. ❖

Left: Bette Davis was a frequent guest on the radio in the Good Old Days.

Punishment?

By Arline Gladman

When I lived on a farm back in the late 1930s and early 1940s, everyone had chores to perform. Age didn't matter; your assignment was geared to your ability. My jobs included mopping the stairs to the second floor on Saturday, which I hated doing, and washing the evening dishes while everyone else did the milking in the barn.

I didn't always carry out my duties according to adult instructions and expectations. What seemed so terribly important to them eluded me at 9 and 10 years old.

My dishwashing especially left much to be desired. I had been educated by the adults to achieve the expected results: "Start with hot, soapy water, and then rub the food particles off of each dish with the dishcloth, beginning with the glasses, utensils, plates, and lastly, the cooking dishes. Rinse and dry."

It sounded simple enough, but it took more time. I was most interested in how fast I could get the supper dishes washed, and then return to play after I had listened to my favorite radio program.

After being warned once, I goofed again. This time I was told I could expect to be punished. "You will not be allowed to listen to *Jack Armstrong, the All-American Boy* for one week."

Before going out to the barn, one of the adults carefully pulled the radio's electric plug.

> *"You will not be allowed to listen to* Jack Armstrong, the All-American Boy *for one week."*

I knew I should just take my punishment, but hearing my program was more important. After all, it was only 15 minutes long, and everyone would be in the barn.

At the time *Jack Armstrong* came on, I plugged the radio into the wall socket. Cautiously watching and listening for anyone coming in, I made sure the volume stayed low and stood almost on top of the radio so that I could hear it.

Then I turned the radio off, pulled the plug from the wall and replaced it precisely as I had found it. I did that all week and never missed a program. But I sure was relieved when the week ended. I had been so scared that I would be caught.

Now, so many years later, I fail to understand why the adults didn't realize I could easily place that plug into the wall. I suppose they thought I paid attention to their warnings about the dangers of electricity. Little did they know!

But I'm convinced the idea worked. I don't remember being punished again for not washing the dishes properly. Just knowing that I could be caught apparently taught me something.

I have never figured out why children think parents wouldn't understand or have never had the same experience. They should realize that parents were children before they became parents, and that they probably solved their difficulties in about the same way.

Of course, parents might never admit it! ❖

Cotton-Pickin' Radio

By Wayne W. Daniel

I wanted a radio more than anything else in the world. But during the Depression, I knew without being told that the family budget could not accommodate such a luxury. While temporarily resigning myself to life without a radio, I determined that my deprivation would be short-lived, and I began thinking of ways to earn money to buy one. Perhaps I could get a job—although, with 8 million unemployed adults in the country, that seemed unlikely. But I kept scheming—and dreaming—about a radio.

In the fall of 1940, when I was 11, my planning bore fruit. I told my parents that I wanted to get a job picking cotton to earn money for a radio. Not only did they approve of the idea, my mother said she would *help* me. When the first cotton bolls opened in the fields of the farmer who had employed us, my mother and I were there with brand-new pick sacks, snatching fluffy locks of white gold from waist-high plants that were reluctant to part with their treasure. Our pay was a penny a pound.

It was a long autumn, but each time I thought of leaving the harvest to folks with stronger backs, visions of that hoped-for radio always inspired me to attack King Cotton with renewed zeal.

By the first of November, the fields of white had turned brown, and no more money was to be made picking cotton. My mother and

I pooled our earnings and went shopping for a radio. We settled on a small, four-tube table model. The clerk said it cost $20, but to my way of thinking, it cost 2,000 pounds of cotton.

My previous exposure to radio had in no way prepared me for the wide range of entertainment and education that I now had at my fingertips. For my pleasure and information there were quiz shows, comedies, music, drama, news, sports and religious programs. I sampled them all and picked favorites on which to bestow my loyalty.

It seemed that I had moved next door to Fibber McGee and Molly, who resided at 79 Wistful Vista. Their neighbors became my neighbors: Mayor LaTrivia; Wallace Wimple and his domineering wife, Sweetie Face; the snobbish Mrs. Uppington; Sis, the precocious brat next door; and the Old-Timer, whose rejoinder to Fibber's every comment was "That's purty good, Johnny, but that ain't the way I heared it."

When Molly squashed her husband's efforts to be cute with an icy "'Tain't funny, McGee," I tended to agree. During every program, I waited with amused anticipation for the inevitable opening of the door to the McGees' overstuffed hall closet and the ensuing rumble as its contents cascaded onto the floor.

Among the quiz programs, *Dr. I.Q.*, "the Mental Banker," was my favorite. When one of the doctor's assistants announced, "I have a gentleman in the balcony, Doctor," I imagined myself to be that gentleman, and I tried hard to correctly answer the doctor's question so I could be the make-believe winner of a few silver dollars rather than the consolation prize of a box of Mars candy bars.

My favorite feature was "that little monument to memory," the Thought Twister. After calling for silence in the audience, the doctor would promise the nervous contestant 35 silver dollars if he or she could "repeat after me exactly as I say it" a dialogue that always followed the same formula. A typical Thought Twister might be, "'The guy is shy,' said Vi to Si. 'The guy is shy, Vi, to her,' said Si."

A typical Thought Twister might be, "'The guy is shy,' said Vi to Si. 'The guy is shy, Vi, to her,' said Si."

In my mind, I rode beside the Lone Ranger and "his faithful Indian companion," Tonto. With the announcer's intonation of "A fiery horse with the speed of light, a cloud of dust and a hearty 'Hi-ho, Silver!'" I was off to help the "daring and resourceful masked rider of the plains … fight for law and order in the early Western United States!"

The momentous events of the 1940s were indelibly impressed on my mind through the words of such radio commentators as Gabriel Heatter, H.V. Kaltenborn and Walter Winchell. When Winchell's staccato voice greeted his listeners with "Good evening, Mr. and Mrs. America, and all the ships at sea. Let's go to press!" I knew that, in terms of drama and suspense, what I was about to hear could not be equaled by the most popular of the fictional programs.

From midmorning until late afternoon, Monday through Friday, the soap operas ruled the airways. I was among that 10 percent of their audience who was male. I was always happy to "Smile awhile with Lorenzo Jones and his wife, Belle."

A mechanic at Jim Barker's garage, the "lovable, impractical" Lorenzo dreamed of becoming a great inventor. Unfortunately, however, such brain-children as the three-spouted teapot—one spout each for strong, medium and weak brews—never quite got off the ground.

One scholar has set the date for the demise of traditional radio programming at Nov. 25, 1960. On that day, four long-running soap operas—*The Second Mrs. Burton, The Right to Happiness, Young Dr. Malone* and *Ma Perkins* went off the air.

Today I have a radio in every room of the house, one in the car, one that I can wear on my belt and listen to through earphones, and one with a handle that I can take to the beach or anywhere else that strikes my fancy.

All of them put together, however, have not brought me one-tenth the pleasure I got from that little four-tube radio that I helped buy in the fall of 1940. ❖

Programs That Changed Our Lives

Chapter Two

To this day I remember the store on Pacific Street, just off Commercial, in the old downtown section of Branson, Mo. Branson, now a booming tourism mecca, was then a sleepy little village. The store was King's Appliance, and it was just a couple of doors down from the studios of KBHM radio station.

I always haunted Pacific Street for the news of the day. You could stand at the front window of KBHM and watch the Associated Press teletype rattle off the latest headlines. I remember a group of us gathered around the Teletype on a cool early evening in late November 1963 trying to read updates as they came off the wire about a shooting in Dallas, Texas.

Just down from the radio station, King's Appliance had a window filled with new televisions. Young and old alike were gathered at the window and inside the store, perched on fenders and crouched at the curbside. Inside, more folks stared in disbelief, trying to absorb the enormity of the loss they were witnessing—a young leader cut down less than three years into his presidency.

Through the years, the airwaves brought us thousands of programs that changed our lives. "Fireside chats" by President Franklin Delano Roosevelt comforted us in the depths of the Great Depression and the crucible of World War II. The news of Japan's surprise attack upon Pearl Harbor horrified and sobered us. Then our spirits were lifted to hear the victory celebrations in New York and Philadelphia after V-J Day. We soared as we watched the first manned space flight of John Glenn in 1962, and again as we watched the snowy pictures from the face of the moon seven years later as Neil Armstrong took that "one small step."

The stories in this chapter will take you back to the days when riding the airwaves was a sometimes bumpy, sometimes scary, sometimes thrilling ride. You'll enjoy the trip as we remember all of those programs—from the monumental to the mundane—that changed our lives back in the Good Old Days.

—*Ken Tate*

The Day Television Changed Our Lives

By Robert W. Hatton

The year was 1954. It was a newsworthy year: Ike was president. The McCarthy spell was finally broken. The Supreme Court ruled that racial segregation must be abolished once and for all in the public schools. Sir Winston Churchill and Herbert Hoover celebrated their 80th birthdays. Through pictures in the United States press, the world—still stunned by the awesome power of the A-bomb—saw for the first time the devastation an H-Bomb could wreak. The 4-minute mile was run by Englishman Robert Bannister and Australian John Landy. Willie Mays led the New York Giants into the World Series where they defeated the Cleveland Indians in four straight games. After a lengthy trial in Cleveland, Ohio, Dr. Sam Sheppard was convicted of the murder of his wife. Ernest Hemingway won the Nobel Prize for Literature.

The rate of inflation in 1954 (as measured by the Consumer Price Index) also made the news; it was a mere one-half of one percent. Prices were comparably low. A gallon of regular gasoline sold for 27 cents. A Plymouth Plaza Club Sedan cost $1,700, and a Packard Clipper was $2,600.

It was on June 25, 1954, that we were married in New York on the NBC television program **Bride and Groom.**

Men's summer suits were $35; women's cotton dresses, $5; and women's and men's dress shoes, $7.95. Paint was $1.99 a gallon. Smoked ham and chuck roast cost 39 cents a pound, while skinless wieners and ground beef went for 3 pounds for $1.

Gerber's baby food was 10 cents a jar. A Brownie Hawkeye camera cost $6.95; a Hoover vacuum cleaner, $12.95; an RCA portable phonograph, $49.95; and a 9.5 cubic foot Kelvinator refrigerator, less than $200. And a 5-cent package of America's favorite drink, Kool-Aid, made two delicious quarts.

It was on June 25, 1954, that the former Marlene Tuller and I, both lifelong residents of Columbus, Ohio, were married in New York City on the NBC daytime television program *Bride and Groom*. The wedding, which was telecast live, took place in a small chapel in the NBC studios.

It all began when we wrote to *Bride and Groom* for an application early in 1953. The long, anxious wait came to an end in May of 1954 with the arrival of a telegram advising us of our selection for the program on Friday, June 25.

The weeks that followed were filled with activity as we completed one form after another, accepted the congratulations of relatives and friends, had several interviews with the local media, and made many preparations for a wedding to be seen by millions.

A few days prior to the date of our wedding, we left for New York City by Greyhound, but in the company of our chaperones, my brother Jerry and Marlene's brother, David.

The author (center) and his bride are pictured in the studio on their big day with John Nelson (left), master of ceremonies, and Phil Hanna, soloist.

The hectic days preceding our wedding included discussions with the program's producers and master of ceremonies, the completion of more legal forms, the acquisition of a New York wedding license, a session with the Baptist minister chosen by the program to perform the marriage (ours was unable to go), a trip to the NBC wardrobe department where Marlene chose her wedding gown from among the hundred or so on display, some sightseeing (it was our first trip to New York), and greeting friends and relatives who came to attend our wedding but whose concerns for the moment were to go to TV game shows and Steve Allen's *Tonight Show*.

We couldn't join them, though, because we had to practice giving the details of our courtship in the few minutes allotted for this on the program. The entire program, including commercials, lasted only 15 minutes. Furthermore, since there were no cue cards and no retakes, we had to memorize a script.

For days we had been trying to convince ourselves that we were ready not only to be married, but to be married on national television as well. When we walked through the doors of NBC at 9 a.m. on Friday, June 25, 1954, the two of us were suddenly aware that there was no way we could ever have been ready for the experience that was awaiting us.

Of course, there was much to keep us busy: television makeup had to be applied; there were pictures to be taken both for our personal use and for publicity purposes; introductions were made all around; and of course, there was the 10:30 a.m. rehearsal, the first and only one.

There was still idle time until the "On-the-Air" sign would light up, however, and we had only to look at the hustle and bustle around us to remind ourselves that ours was not going to be any ordinary wedding. Products to be promoted during the commercial breaks were being put into place, television camera operators were deciding on the best vantage points from which to film, TV monitors (a couple of which were close enough that we could watch ourselves being married on television) were strategically placed, and the master of ceremonies, soloist and harpist were rehearsing their respective parts in the program. And everywhere there were clocks and lights to remind us that we had only so long to say things and to look in a certain direction when speaking.

What kind of story did two 20-year-olds tell on national television moments before they exchanged wedding vows? It focused on my choice of a location to propose to Marlene. We were on a Ferris wheel, and I waited until we reached the highest point to ask her to marry me. I had plenty of time to say things in just the right way because we were stuck there for a few moments due to a mechanical failure. Perhaps it was only a coincidence, but the moment Marlene accepted my proposal, the wheel started turning again. Or was it my head that was spinning?

John Nelson, master of ceremonies, and Phil Hanna, soloist, did everything they could to put us at ease both before and during the program. (Our timing was thrown off for a moment, however, when Phil missed John's cue and was a few seconds late in bringing our rings from off-camera to show on television.) They were especially adept at picking up the slack when we stumbled over an occasional line.

Perhaps we were all a bit relieved when our wedding ceremony was over, and after one last commercial break, we and our television audience were told that we would be spending our honeymoon at the resort in Bedford Springs, Pa. Our trip there and back was to be made in a new 1954 Pontiac made available to us for this purpose. All of this was compliments of *Bride and Groom*. We were also given our wedding rings, a variety of household appliances and furnishings, and a 16mm sound film (this was long before the advent of videotape) of the entire program.

Our friends and relatives rejoiced with us in our marriage and our instant celebrity status as a couple married on national television. It was some time, however, before we could convince some people that the real wedding was not performed in a second, off-camera ceremony.

This exciting, never-to-be-forgotten period of our lives ended some 10 days after it all began as we stepped down from our Greyhound bus in Columbus. Marlene returned to her job at Nationwide Insurance Co. while I resumed my studies in Spanish education at Capital University.

Perhaps our years together would have been no different had we not appeared on that *Bride and Groom* program in 1954. There is no way of knowing, of course, but it was a magical moment that we're certainly glad that we were privileged to enjoy. It was also the day that television changed our lives. ❖

Radio Was King

By Russ Barrick

My mother knew only two chords on the guitar, but that was enough to get my oldest brother, Jim, interested. It was right after the Depression, and money was still hard to come by. But my parents went ahead and ordered a guitar through the Spiegel mail-order house—$13, including case. My other brother, Romey, and I felt a little left out, so they got us a couple of mandolins.

We played at many civic functions around Martinsville, our hometown, but more than anything else, we must have played at more than 300 amateur shows during a seven-year period. Amateur shows were very popular back then because all of the talent was local.

In the spring of 1933, Blocks Department Store in Indianapolis sponsored a talent show on Saturday mornings on WFBM. Many people in town decided that the Barrick brothers should enter the contest. Our parents were very excited.

We did enter, and we played *Home on the Range*. Listeners voted by sending in penny postcards. We won, getting 6,500 votes in a town of about 4,500 people!

The prize was a big angel food cake that was decorated, appropriately enough, with miniature radio aerials on top. We displayed the cake in the candy case of our local grocery store for a few days. Needless to say, we were very proud.

Radio was king back then, and it gave my brothers and me an opportunity to become local celebrities.

My brother Jim passed away in 1947 as he piloted a plane in the Air Force Reserves at Stout Field in Indianapolis. My brother Romey passed away in 1996. He was retired from the Air Force. I am 75 years old—and I still play the guitar and mandolin. ❖

Bride and Groom

By Jan Holden

Weddings have been performed in every imaginable place—aboard ships and planes, in hospital rooms, even on the golf course. Don and Dee Huston of Greenville, S.C., exchanged their vows on ABC's popular radio program *Bride and Groom* on July 14, 1949.

Don had heard of the *Bride and Groom* radio show and decided to send for their contest rules and an application. It was more of a light-hearted whim at the time, but when the application arrived, he and Dee met at a local coffee shop and filled out the details of their meeting and courtship. They sent the information off with a photograph and put it out of their minds.

But ABC didn't. They liked the clean-cut good looks of the Iowa couple. They enjoyed their humor and frankness. They enjoyed the story of Don, a high-school basketball star, who met Dee, a pretty cheerleader from a nearby town. They reveled in the fact that their fathers were competitors, both managing rural retail lumberyards. It was pure Americana.

The wedding was to be on June 26. Family and friends were notified. Dee had her gown, and Don had the minister booked. Then the telegram arrived—a very official-looking telegram stating that Deloris Hess and Don Huston had been chosen to be married over national radio. The only hook was that the wedding date had to be changed to July 14.

The family agreed to take a vote as to when and where the wedding would take place. Would Don and Dee have their small-town wedding? Or would they travel 3,000 miles to Los Angeles and deliver their vows before an audience numbering in the thousands?

After considerable discussion, the votes were cast. All but two voted for the radio wedding.

A very official-looking telegram stated that they had been chosen to be married over national radio.

Of course, the "no" votes were cast by Don and Dee's mothers.

Don put $400 down on a new Ford, and with their maid of honor, they set off to drive to California. Don's brother, Jack, who was going to be the best man, drove out with their kid sisters. They all stayed with friends of Don's folks along the way.

Dee had brought her own wedding gown and was determined to wear it, despite the fact that the folks at *Bride and Groom* offered her one that had been worn in *Gone With the Wind*. It was comforting for the nervous bride to have something she had chosen herself for the big day. Even more comforting was the arrival of several friends who just couldn't miss out on Don and Dee's wedding.

When Don and Dee arrived at the Chapman Park Hotel in Hollywood, they were greeted warmly by the program's host, John Nelson. John interviewed the pair concerning their meeting and courtship, focusing on some of the silly and sentimental things most couples treasure. He also ran off a list of wonderful prizes to be awarded to Don and Dee at the end of the program. Among the gifts were a weeklong honeymoon, sterling watches, rings, luggage, dishes, silver service and even a cocker spaniel pup! It seemed the sponsors had thought of everything!

After the 30-minute program, Don and Dee were whisked away to a wedding chapel where they exchanged their vows and were pronounced man and wife. *Bride and Groom's* John Nelson got in line with the others to kiss the bride.

The *Bride and Groom* radio program ran for five years, from 1945–1950, and more than a thousand couples delivered their "I do's" to a national listening audience. Looking back, Don and Dee think they made the right choice by having a radio wedding. ❖

A Wunnerful Afternoon

By Glen Herndon

Lawrence Welk, arguably America's most beloved bandleader of the Big Band era and beyond, showed me firsthand in Detroit many years ago what a considerate man he was, and how carefully he oversaw details of his appearances.

I was a staff photographer in 1959 at the Chrysler Corp. Lawrence Welk's television show was sponsored by Dodge. When he came to town, it was always a public relations event.

I had lunch with him, little Janet Lennon and her father, and a young champion drummer from Lawrence Welk's newly formed youth orchestra.

The one picture I kept from that day shows him and little Janet, age 9. I didn't have to do a thing but point and shoot. Lawrence Welk set up the shot and said, "Ready when you are."

Later, on the stage of the Masonic Hall, they rehearsed his trademark polka with Janet and the orchestra, which was made up of local pros from the Musician's Union Hall reading Lawrence Welk's arrangements. They were practicing for a gala Junior Achievement concert.

After the polka rehearsal, Welk asked the local bandleader what kind of drums they had for his young champion drummer to use for his number. The bandleader said, "Oh, but didn't you know? One of our local Junior Achievement youngsters is scheduled to do a solo on Benny Goodman's *Sing, Sing, Sing*."

I waited to see if Lawrence Welk would make a scene. He got a little red in the face

May 7, 1959. Lawrence Welk and Janet Lennon at the Detroit Sheraton-Cadillac Hotel Junior Achievement luncheon.

for just a moment, but he came right back with what I thought was very calm and reasoned judgment.

He motioned for his young drummer to come over for a conference. I distinctly heard him say, "You heard the man. I hate to deny you, but you are a champion and will have many concerts in the spotlight. This night will probably be the greatest moment this local boy will know in a long time. Did you bring your tap-dancing shoes?"

"Yes," the boy said. "I brought them along in my bag."

"Then put them on. Can you tap to *Cherry Pink and Apple-Blossom White*?"

"I think so. It's one of my favorite tunes."

Then Welk asked the bandleader, "You have my 'sheets' for that one?"

"Yes sir!"

"Then let's try it."

Soon the boy was at center stage. The band struck up the music, but after a few seconds, Lawrence Welk yelled, "*Hold it*! Hold it! We can't hear the boy's taps. We've got to cut this thing back!"

He worked diligently with the bandleader for a long while, cutting out parts and reducing the band to a mere skeleton of the arrangement— but you could hear the loud tapping echoing through that big hall. Lawrence Welk smiled; he was satisfied.

I only covered the rehearsal, but reports circulating the next day amongst my friends at Dodge public relations indicated that it was probably the best-received Junior Achievement concert ever. ❖

Of Mars and Men

By Thomas A. Luckenbach

To say we were hoaxed is to understate the matter. Now we laugh about it, but that night, we cried. A Sunday evening radio broadcast started it all: a retelling of H.G. Wells' *The War of the Worlds*, presented by Orson Welles. His was a novel approach: repeated interruptions of a program of dance music with a series of simulated news bulletins.

Reported first were some violent explosions on the surface of Mars seen by a Chicago observatory; then, that a huge metal cylinder had landed on a farm in Grover's Mills, N.J. The relayed news bulletins gave way to live, on-the-spot reports by excited announcers telling abut strange creatures emerging from the large cylinder. Soon widespread death and destruction were reported throughout New Jersey from the invader's death rays and poison gases.

It was Oct. 30, 1938, and what had been intended as Halloween entertainment proved to be far from entertaining to millions of people across the country, for many did not pay attention to the program's introduction, which stated that CBS was presenting *The Mercury Theatre on the Air* with Orson Welles in *The War of the Worlds*. Nor did they question the plausibility of what they heard,

"Oh, my gosh! They're attacking us!" Mom shrieked.

for radio, till then, had been a trusted friend whose credibility was unquestioned. Consequently, they believed that a devastating attack was indeed occurring.

Not us. We learned about the supposed invasion from a breathless young cousin sent to fetch us to my grandmother's house a block away. Words spilled from him in gasping spurts: "There's some kind of invasion in New Jersey! … People are dying! … Hurry to Grandma's house! … The whole family is there!"

Dad said we would come immediately. Then he sent my cousin back to the gathered family.

My sister El and I put on coats and hats, and waited quietly near the kitchen door. Dad banked the fire in the coal-burning stove, and Mom said she would switch off the lights and lock the doors.

As she crossed the dimly lit parlor to lock the front door, Mom was startled by a loud engine roar that pierced the dark night's quiet. Suddenly, a high-pitched squeal mingled with the roar, filling us with terror. The squeal ended abruptly with a loud crash outside our door, sending a tremor through the house. But the engine roar persisted, louder than ever.

"Oh, my gosh! They're attacking us!" Mom shrieked as she recoiled from the door and the terrifying noise.

Dad rushed to the front door with El and me, wide-eyed, in his wake. Mom's shout-whisper stopped him short of opening the door: "Don't! What if … ?" But her admonition was cut short by the sudden silencing of the engine.

In the silence that followed, Mom and Dad tiptoed to a window and nervously peeked out, but they could discern little in the darkness. But as their eyes adjusted to the dark, fear colored their interpretation of the sight: a large, shadowy figure lying motionless against the front steps. Too frightened to leave, they stared unbelievingly at the thing before them.

Suddenly it began to move. Awkwardly, the ill-defined shape slowly transformed before their eyes. As shadow became substance, two were now where one had been: a large, helmeted creature and a machine with shiny spoked discs at each end.

The creature clumsily rose and looked furtively about. Suddenly our visitor deftly jerked the recumbent machine upright and pushed it back through the gap it had made in the hedge. Then and only then did Mom and Dad realize that they were not under attack; that we were safe; that we were the victims of a cruel coincidence.

Regardless of the happenings in New Jersey, our front-yard invasion in Pennsylvania was a sham; the "invader" was a drunken motorcyclist, and the driver was now fleeing to avoid arrest.

As the motor's sound receded, El and I rushed to Mom and Dad for comfort and reassurance. Dad held the three of us in a tight embrace, nervously laughing about how we had been deceived and wondering aloud whether our porch had been damaged.

"I'm hot. Can we go to Grandma's now?" I chirped from the center of our hugging family.

"Oh, my gosh! We have to get to Grandma's. Let's go!"

People fearing for their lives and thinking they were under attack prepared to defend themselves and their property.

Outside, we paused briefly to examine the porch. Fortunately it was not damaged. Only the bent hedge and scuff marks on the ground testified that anything had happened at all.

Minutes later, we were climbing Grandma's back porch steps. We were met by a cluster of somber teenage cousins and uncles with a strategic mission: surveillance of our valley's eastern ridge for any early signs of invaders.

We entered Grandma's kitchen, where El and I joined our younger cousins who sat around in uncharacteristic, awe-struck silence. Mom and Dad went on into the dining room where the adults surrounded a table-model radio. Heads turned to nod wordless greetings, then turned back to stare uncomprehendingly, some at the radio, some at the floor, but none at one another.

Another cylinder had just been reported near Morristown. Again, fearsome creatures emerged—and they appeared to be heading toward New York City.

That triggered an outburst from Mom: "Oh, my gosh! That's where my kid sister Betty lives!" Then she began to cry.

Airborne military personnel, we were told, had sighted the invaders near Bayonne, and while trying to bomb them, were themselves destroyed by heat rays. An estimated 3 million frantic people were reportedly evacuating Manhattan to evade the black, poisonous gas spreading before the invaders.

Picturing in her mind the terrible scenes, Mom sobbed: "Oh, Betty, Betty …"

The silence thus disrupted, others began murmuring questions: "What should we do? What can we do?"

"Let's get out of here while we can."

"But where can we go?"

"We can't go anywhere right now. We don't have a car."

"Well, we should do something. We can't just sit here and be poisoned."

On and on it went until someone blurted, "At least if we die, we'll all die together!"

At that regrettable statement, the women and children began crying in a long overdue emotional explosion. Our wails drowned out the radio. Perhaps to disguise his own inner turmoil, an uncle bellowed that we were "a bunch of cry-babies" and demanded silence in simple terms: "Darn it! I can't hear the radio! Be quiet!"

Order restored, we again listened intently, but what we now heard was confusing—no more reports of landings, attacks, annihilation. Instead, a Professor Richard Pearson talked about the matter—not as if it were happening, but as if it had happened at some time in the past. Soon he finished, his closing words followed by a musical interlude.

Then we heard: "This is Orson Welles, ladies and gentlemen, out of character to assure you that *The War of the Worlds* has no further significance than as the holiday offering it was intended to be: the *Mercury Theatre's* own radio version of dressing up in a sheet and saying 'Boo.' Starting now, we couldn't soap all your windows and steal all your garden gates by tomorrow, so we did the best next thing. We annihilated the world before your very ears and utterly destroyed the CBS. You will be relieved, I hope, to learn that both institutions are still open for business.

"So, goodbye, everybody, and remember, please, for the next day or so, the terrible lesson you learned tonight: That grinning, glowing, globular invader of your living room is an inhabitant of the pumpkin patch. And if your doorbell rings and nobody's there, that was no Martian—it's Halloween!"

Slowly, the message penetrated our fear-numbed brains. And then we realized we'd been had. "It was all a joke!"

"No! They couldn't pull a trick like that on the radio!"

"Well, they did. You heard him plain as day."

"Oh, my gosh! And here we are worrying and crying like a bunch of fools."

Smiles tinged with embarrassment appeared around the room, but recovery was slow. The tension was still almost tangible. One uncle had a remedy: "Hey, Mom, we need a drink."

"Good idea," said Grandma with a smile. "I'll bring some glasses. Someone pour some soda for the kids. They ain't never been so quiet!"

Indeed, we had been quiet, but quickly our mood changed from somber to festive.

Soon the mood changed in the dining room, too, as the rye worked its magic: Ease replaced tension, anxiety yielded to calm. Now the motorcycle incident could be told and its humorous side appreciated. Before the spirits took full command, however, someone noticed the time and clearer heads prevailed. It was late, and the kids had to be put to bed.

Orson Welles on the air.

So coats were donned, goodbyes said, and with a trailing wake of laughter, we wearily trudged home. And weary we were, though not so much from the hour—it was after 11 p.m.—as from the range and intensity of emotion we had experienced. In a scant two hours, we had plunged to unfathomed depths of terror and raised to heights of giddy glee.

Thanks to Martians, motorcycles and Orson Welles, we would long remember that night and ever appreciate the meaning of "trick" in the Halloween expression "trick or treat." ❖

Martian Invasion!

By Anita Hunter

The night before Halloween, Oct. 30, 1938, my mother, father and I were driving on the highway from Jersey City to Englewood, N.J. We were returning home from a speech Dad had given on his specialty, safety education.

That subject was not very interesting to me, a 14-year-old, but as soon as we tuned in the car radio to the Edgar Bergen-Charlie McCarthy show, I was wide awake. I wanted to be sure to remember Charlie's jokes to tell my new friends at Dwight Morrow High School the next day.

We had just moved East from a small Midwestern town, and this larger school was quite an adjustment. I was eager to try to fit in.

As I sat in the backseat of our Chevy, laughing along with my folks and the studio audience, Dad commented, "I've never seen such a deserted road, not even out in the country back in Iowa. There hasn't been a single car for the last half-hour."

Little did we know that on another radio station, Orson Welles' *Mercury Theatre on the Air* was broadcasting H.G. Wells' *War of the Worlds*. All over the United States, people listened spellbound as reports came in that a meteorite had landed near Princeton, N.J. According to the tale, strange beings—the vanguard of an invading army from Mars—were advancing along the very highway we were traveling.

The official-sounding voice of the secretary of the interior affirmed the gravity of the situation. He urged calm, resourceful action as evacuation instructions were given for Newark.

Urgent bulletins followed: "The Army, Air Force and all defenses are wiped out! Martian vehicles are reported landing in Buffalo … in Chicago … in St. Louis!" Supposedly, black, poisonous smoke was pouring over the New Jersey flatlands. "The invaders are entering New York City. … Panicked citizens are trying to flee!"

A final report came from an on-the-spot reporter: "They're falling like flies. … The smoke is crossing Fifth Avenue. … They're 100 yards away! … 50 feet! …"

Then—silence.

Listeners deserted their radios to pray, to run into the streets, or to jump into their cars to escape. In doing so, they missed the announcement: "After a brief intermission, *The Mercury Theatre on the Air* will continue with our presentation of H.G. Wells' *War of the Worlds*."

Telephone lines across the nation jammed as many frantic Americans tried to call authorities or reach their loved ones for a final farewell.

Telephone lines were jammed as frantic Americans tried to call authorities or reach loved ones.

Mom, Dad and I went to bed soon after we arrived at our apartment in Englewood. The next day, near my locker at school, two girls were engrossed in a copy of the morning newspaper. "Did you listen to the radio last night?" one of them asked.

At last I had an opportunity to tell them about Charlie McCarthy's latest quips. But before I could answer, one girl thrust the newspaper into my hand. The words leaped off the front page: "Martians … local highway … invasion … panic all over the United States."

"I was on that road last night!" I gasped. Soon I was surrounded by amazed, questioning students who asked if I actually had seen any Martians, or wild-eyed people with shotguns, or auto wrecks, or burned-out, smoking buildings.

And so Orson Welles and I were launched. He had a sponsor within a week—and I was nominated for class secretary a few days later. ❖

Princess for a Day

By Faye Whatley Thompson

Radio was the primary source of home entertainment in the 1930s and 1940s. No home was without a radio unless the family could not afford to buy one. When my older sister, Linda, age 10, and I heard that a new radio station was coming to our hometown of Americus, Ga., we were elated. We loved to sing, and we knew most of the popular songs by heart, as well as the hymns and choruses at our church. We always sang at family reunions with just a little coercion from family members.

There was a rumor that the new station, WDEC, would offer a weekly talent show for children. We began watching for the starting date, and we prepared for the event. We could hardly wait.

The station manager, Charlie Smith, finally announced that the new program would air each Saturday morning from 10–11 a.m. Johnny Smoker, an announcer at WDEC, was to be the emcee, and a local pianist would be on hand to practice with any children who arrived early.

Linda and I woke up bright and early each Saturday, and with sheet music in hand, walked to the radio station just a block from our house. We sang popular songs such as *The Old Lamplighter, Stardust, Linda, Moonlight and Roses, Tea for Two, Peg o' My Heart* and *You Belong to Me*. We also sang many of our favorite Irish tunes such as *My Wild Irish Rose, Mother MacRee* and *When Irish Eyes Are Smiling*.

> *The prize package included a flight over the city in a private plane and a free lunch at a popular restaurant.*

As a promotional gimmick, the station gave a new ballpoint pen—the latest and greatest invention of the day—to each participant. So not only did we get a new ballpoint pen, but we got to sing on the radio every week with other promising young musicians. It was quite an honor to participate, and winning a prize was icing on the cake.

For a limited time, the station sponsored a Prince and Princess for a Day contest. Each week after the final contestant had performed, the contestants and studio audience voted for a winner. The "audience" in the cramped, standing-room-only studio consisted mainly of parents, relatives and friends of the participants, so the winners were usually those who had brought along the most people to vote for them.

Two winners, a boy and a girl, were crowned Prince and Princess for a Day. Their special prize package included a flight over the city in a private plane and a free lunch of their choosing at The Varsity, a popular restaurant and student hangout near the local community college.

The two lucky winners were wrapped in royal "robes"—actually polka-dot cotton bathrobes, but to the winners they might as well have been purple velvet. The princess received a corsage of carnations, and

The author (right) and James Jennings eat together in the restaurant after winning the titles of Prince and Princess for a Day.

the prince, a boutonniere. Linda won before I did, and when she shared the details of her exhilarating experience with me, it made me want to win even more.

As fate would have it, a few weeks later, with the help of my father and his fellow co-workers from the furniture store, I was crowned Princess for a Day. And what a wonderful, exciting day it was for a skinny little girl!

James Jennings, a local boy who was a few years my junior, was crowned the prince. Our picture was taken while we ate in the restaurant, and copies of the photo were given to us as mementos of the occasion.

If I had to choose a most exciting experience from my childhood, it probably would be the thrill of being crowned Princess for a Day.

Eventually, due to the program's popularity and the lack of space in the studio, the show was moved to a larger room in the historic Windsor Hotel, and later, to an even larger auditorium above the Carnegie Library on Jackson Street. We now had a stage, which gave a more professional flair to the program.

But while the talent show continued for a while, the Prince and Princess for a Day contest was discontinued.

When Daddy became the manager of the new Little's Furniture Store, he persuaded the store owners to sponsor another radio talent contest. It was held in the old Rylander Theater. The prize for first place was a whopping $10,

and second place was $5—not bad for that time. Winners were selected by a sound meter that measured the audience's applause. And so the number of family members present once again played a big role in the final outcome.

Linda and I sang quite a few solos in that contest. Like the other contestants, we were anxious to win the big prize, but we were not so fortunate. We were defeated by talented young dancers, guitarists and pianists. Singers were a dime a dozen, and only exceptional singers took home the prizes.

When Linda was 12 and I was 10, we decided to give it one more try by singing a duet. We worked faithfully on our song, *Now Is the Hour*, until we felt we were accomplished enough to win. When we finally did sing our duet, we won second place. A cute and very talented 4-year-old boy who played the guitar was the winner. Not long after that, the show closed.

As fate would have it, television soon became the center of many homes, and radio faded into the background. But my memories of those fabulous days of radio are good ones, forever etched in my mind.

Neither my sister nor I ever launched a successful career in music, but in our senior years, we still enjoy singing. When I sing an occasional solo in our church choir, I relish the sensation of a worthwhile accomplishment—a sensation that, without a doubt, I first experienced back in the Good Old Days of radio. ❖

Lights! Action!

By Wendy Hobday Haugh

Watching black-and-white television was a stellar experience in the 1950s. But bigger still was the thrill of actually appearing on television, as I did on my 4th birthday in February 1957. *The Freddy Freihofer Show*, as we kids dubbed it, aired live on weekdays from 4:45–5 p.m., 52 weeks of the year, for 17 glorious years (1949–1966). Sponsored by the local Freihofer Baking Co., *Breadtime Stories*, as it was officially called, gave birthday boys and girls a chance to celebrate their special day on television, complete with yummy baked goods and a spirited commercial artist/emcee.

Dressed as a company deliveryman, the emcee enchanted us by telling stories that he illustrated on a gigantic sketchpad. Wearing white paper birthday hats bearing the distinctive Freihofer script, we kids sat on wooden bleachers, enthralled by the lights and action of a real live television production at WRGB in Schenectady, N.Y.

> *The show gave birthday boys and girls a chance to celebrate their special day on television.*

I will never forget that day. Dressed in a brand-new pair of pink patent-leather shoes (to date, my fanciest shoes ever) and a pink, puffy-sleeved party dress with black velvet trim, I felt like a fairy princess. In contrast to the dresses passed down to me from my older cousins—and the play clothes passed down to me from my big brother—my crisp, ultra-feminine outfit added a touch of magic to an already wondrous, wintry afternoon.

Although snacks and stories abounded, the real highlight of the program came when the emcee called out, "Whooooo wants to … squiggle?" Instantly, the air was filled with excited squeals: "I do! I do!" A child was handed a crayon and invited to draw a quick squiggle on the emcee's supersized pad. Given that ever-so-simple line, curlicue or dot, the emcee was then challenged to draw a specific object of the child's choice.

Anything under the sun was fair game. But as hard as we kids tried to stump him with offbeat requests, to our utter amazement, the clever artist always successfully completed his mission.

Adding to the sweetness of the event, the Freihofer Baking Co. provided each birthday youngster with a lavish cake of his or her dreams.

I will never, ever forget my cake. It was the most spectacular, innovative cake on display! An 8-inch plastic doll stood buried in the cake's center with just her head of blond curls showing above the lacy, swirling white frosting that formed her exquisite gown.

The author celebrated her 4th birthday in February 1957 by appearing with other birthday youngsters on a live broadcast at the television studio of WRGB, Schenectady, N.Y. She is sitting in the center of the front row, wearing the black-trimmed dress. Her cake, with the doll's head visible, is in the center of the front row.

I had never before—nor have I ever since—seen such a beautiful cake. My only letdown came hours later, when my mother carefully cut and served slices to family members. By dessert's end, I was sobbing uncontrollably. "What's the matter, honey?" Mom asked, clearly alarmed.

"My doll is naked!" I cried in dismay. "We ate her dress!"

Thirty years later, I was privileged to meet the emcee and ask him a few questions about his success on The Freddy Freihofer Show. To my surprise, he took no credit whatsoever for the show's long and successful run.

"It was all you kids, Wendy," he insisted. "You were genuine, full of enthusiasm, spontaneity and natural curiosity. That's what made things click."

Until that day, I had harbored a 4-year-old's perspective on a delightful childhood experience. But after bumping into "Uncle Jim," as I'd known him long ago, I found myself glowing anew. Intuitively, and ever so generously, the man had shed new light on a precious memory by telling me that we kids had actually carried the show.

Turns out, the squiggles weren't the highlight after all. ❖

The Davis Sisters

By Olivia Eubanks

My dad bought me a used guitar in 1939. It was smaller than most guitars, and it had the name *May-Bel* across the front. Some people thought that it might have once belonged to Maybelle Carter, but no one could prove it. It didn't matter; I was delighted! I practiced diligently until the blisters on my fingers became calluses. I acquired a limited ability to strum the guitar, and I could sing along with it.

Later on, I bought a larger used guitar and began playing and singing in different places. It was fun, but I wanted more.

In the early 1940s, radio station KGRH was set up in Fayetteville, Ark. The broadcast studio was just a small room off the lobby of a local hotel. In it were microphones, a grand piano, a table and some chairs.

The author with her guitar, circa 1946.

At the top of a large glass window was a signal light that remained green until someone was "on the air," at which point the light turned red. Large maroon drapes were pulled closed across the studio window, except when an audience had assembled to watch the performers.

One day I walked into the studio, confronted a dark-eyed man who said his name was Nick, and asked if I could sing on the radio. He replied, "Well, let's see what you've got."

When I strummed my guitar and sang, he seemed to like it, and right then and there, he gave me a 15-minute program on Saturday mornings.

I chose a theme song called *Sing When the Birds Are Waking*. Nick introduced me to his wife, Cathy, a pretty, blue-eyed blonde who often did the announcing.

One day when I was due to sing, Cathy approached me holding a huge baby. Shoving the baby into my arms, she said, "Hold my nephew." Then she rushed into the studio to do her announcing.

The squirming baby was heavy and hard to hold. By the time his mother came and took him from me, I was nervous and sweaty. I picked up my guitar and rushed into the studio just as Cathy was beginning to announce my show. With a fast-beating heart, I watched the red light come on a few seconds before I was to sing

The Davis Sisters, 1945 (left to right): the author, Bettye and Mary Jo.

my theme song. I sang a couple of lines, and Cathy announced my program.

After a little while, my sisters, Bettye and Mary Jo, joined me on the program. We had a more melodious sound as a group, and we called ourselves The Davis Sisters. Sometimes we each sang a solo, and then sang in harmony. Mary Jo and I often sang duets.

Soon we were being asked to sing for the Veterans of Foreign Wars and hospitalized World War II veterans. It was 1945. The war had ended. President Franklin Delano Roosevelt was dead, and Harry S. Truman, the former vice president, was now president.

At one of our programs at the veterans hospital, we were asked to help the veterans who were playing bingo. I helped one blind patient by reading the numbers to him and playing his numbers when they were called. Bettye and Mary Jo were helping a young

man with bandaged hands who told us they had been damaged by jungle rot. He really liked Mary Jo, so for Christmas that year, he gave her a beautiful doll and a cute, blue silk kimono. With her straight black hair and gray-green eyes, she looked very pretty in it.

The following year, a photographer came to the radio station and asked The Davis Sisters to pose for a picture. They didn't want a guitar in the picture, but we were already lined up to sing *Down in the Valley*.

As time passed, we sang in empty school-houses with other bands. When I married in 1948, Mary Jo sang at my wedding. Later, when my sisters married, we continued to sing, but we were no longer known as The Davis Sisters.

Sister Bettye has passed on, so Mary Jo and I are the only ones sharing the memories of our good old music-making days on KGRH. ❖

A Beginning Never to Be Forgotten

By Faith Fifield

Have you ever gathered around a radio to listen to the president talk about what was happening? Well, I did, in my father's house in Bell Gardens, a suburb of Los Angeles, on Dec. 8, 1941, when I was but a child. And so did many of our neighbors. This day would never be forgotten.

In 1941, few people had radios, and those who did shared with their neighbors. Doors and windows were never locked. People visited one another and shared everything—food, clothes and work.

Dad bought a used upright radio from a furniture store for a fraction of what it was worth. He was a horse trader from way back. He traded with the best.

He came home with the radio in the back of the landlord's pickup truck. They unloaded the radio and carried it into the front room. Then Dad went around to the neighbors and invited them over to listen to President Franklin D. Roosevelt's speech. His speeches were normally called "Fireside Chats," but this one was set in the early afternoon, Washington, D.C., time.

In a split second, the history of the world had changed, and so had our own history.

President Roosevelt would deliver the special speech at 9:30 a.m., Pacific time, locally over radio station KNX. We took it for granted that the speech would be about the meetings being held in Washington, D.C., with the Japanese ambassador concerning peace talks between our country and Japan. The outcome of these talks affected all of us, so we were interested in any news of these proceedings.

Dad invited Evaline and Joe Shore next door, Mamie and Alfred Gingrich across the street, and Ike and Grace Fredricks from farther on down the street.

Mom made a tall urn of coffee and baked a batch of apple crumb sweet rolls. The house smelled of aromatic coffee, fresh apples and pungent spices. My job was to dust the furniture and set out coffee cups and dessert plates.

At 9 o'clock, as the neighbors began to arrive, Mom moved the coffee pot from the stove to the kitchen table. Dad greeted Alfred

Facing page: President Franklin D. Roosevelt (1882–1945) sits at his radio desk in the White House, Washington, D.C., on New Year's Day, 1940. His leg braces, seldom seen in photographs, are visible in this image. Getty Images.

and Mamie as they came through the front door. "Al, good to see you. Mamie, you're still a pretty little thing."

Mamie was a young woman in her early 20s and blushed very easily. Dad and Al laughed. Mamie scurried into the kitchen where Mother was. Dad and Al continued talking about the work they were doing with the WPA—a common topic for the day.

Just about then, Joe, Evaline and their three girls arrived. The girls and I scampered to my bedroom and my toy chest. Evaline joined the women in the kitchen. The men gathered in the front room to admire the radio. Dad turned it on and fiddled with the dials.

The girls and I played pickup sticks until Mom called us into the living room to hear the broadcast from President Roosevelt. A lot of strange noises were coming from the radio—static. Dad kept twisting the dials. The radio was his new toy.

Ike and Grace had arrived while we were in my bedroom. Ike asked, "How about some coffee, Ham?" Hamblin was our surname, and "Ham" was my Dad's nickname. Everyone called him that.

"Gloria, bring in some coffee and rolls," Dad said to Mom.

"Let me give you a hand," Evaline joined in. "After all, four hands are better than two." Both women went back into the kitchen. Neighbors were friendly like this—always giving a helping hand where needed.

Joe, Ike and Al sat in the three big easy chairs and left the rocker for Dad. Mamie and Grace sat on the sofa in front of the big bay window overlooking Darwell Avenue. Mom carried in the coffee urn and rolls, and set them down on the coffee table. Evaline had the cups and dessert plates. Everyone helped himself or herself except for Dad, and Mom served him.

All of us turned our attention to the voice coming over the radio. There was crackling and popping of static, and then a voice came in clearly. After a few comprehensible words,

Most of our fleet had been in the harbor at the time of the attack, and it had sustained heavy damage.

though, the voice faded. It was faint for a few minutes. We kept listening, hoping it would become clear again so that we could hear the words. The women were silent. The men kept advising Dad about what to do with the dials.

As the sound became audible again, we could tell that this voice belonged to President Roosevelt. He had a dynamic way of speaking—almost mesmerizing. He announced that Japan had bombed Pearl Harbor the previous morning, Dec. 7.

Everyone drew in a deep breath. President Roosevelt went on to say that this was a dastardly deed done at a time when Japan's ambassador was in meetings talking peace.

At the same time, Japan attacked an American port without notice, declaring war by their actions.

Hundreds of Americans had been killed and many more had been injured. Most of our fleet had been in the harbor at the time of the attack, and it had sustained heavy damage. Facilities on the main island were damaged or demolished.

To this point, we had been neutral in the World War that began in the late 1930s when Germany invaded Poland. Now we would be in the middle of the soup. The only thing left for us to do was declare war on Japan and possibly on Germany and Italy.

Everyone began talking at once, except for us kids. When the president continued, the room hushed. "With confidence in our armed forces—with the unbounding determination of our people—we will gain the inevitable triumph—so help us God."

Our excitement over having a radio was completely forgotten. In a split second, the history of the world had changed, and so had our own history.

I'll never forget that day. Few people who lived through it did. I remember the excitement over the radio, the good neighbors and the number of those neighbors who died later. And President Roosevelt's words were never forgotten. This was the beginning of World War II for America. All of us remember Pearl Harbor. ❖

Calling Captain Midnight

By Mel Tharp

Beginning with Pearl Harbor on Dec. 7, 1941, and the United States' subsequent entry into World War II, "total mobilization" was the order of the day. Madison Avenue quickly answered the call to arms. "Lucky Strike Green has gone to war!" became a battle cry of the American Tobacco Co. Hollywood turned out war movies in clusters, and radio soon followed suit.

Cowboy movie star Tom Mix, in one of his radio segments, took time out from fighting cattle rustlers long enough to go on a mission to Tokyo for the OSS. The problems of Tom's mission were exacerbated by the fact that his Western features made him stand out in a crowd. This, however, proved to be a minor problem. A little walnut stain served to dye the skin, and with the help of a bit of transparent tape, it was a simple matter to give Tom's eyes more of an Oriental appearance. To most of us youngsters in the radio audience, it seemed like a very clever idea. (Obviously we weren't as sophisticated as most of today's children.)

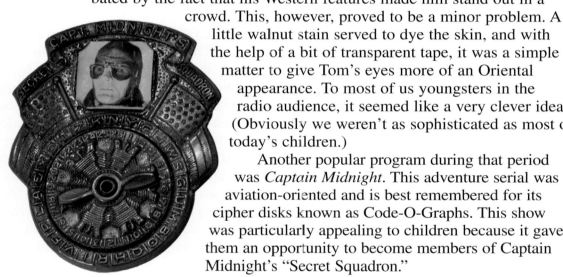

A Captain Midnight's Secret Squadrom decoder pin.

Another popular program during that period was *Captain Midnight*. This adventure serial was aviation-oriented and is best remembered for its cipher disks known as Code-O-Graphs. This show was particularly appealing to children because it gave them an opportunity to become members of Captain Midnight's "Secret Squadron."

The show was sponsored by Ovaltine, and membership in the Secret Squadron was obtained by sending in a seal from an Ovaltine container. In return, the member received a Code-O-Graph cipher disk. (Today these are prized collectibles, selling for $35–$75.)

To me and several others in my sixth-grade class, *Captain Midnight* episodes ranked second only to the latest war news in the order of "serious business."

At first, my classmates and I were satisfied to root from the sidelines, but then we started to feel left out of the action. At the close of each program, an announcer conducted a "signal search" involving an encrypted message about some element of the following episode was broadcast. To enter this inner circle of people privy to "classified information," we decided to become members and form our own unit of the Secret Squadron.

About three weeks after sending off our Ovaltine labels, we received our membership cards and the Code-O-Graph disks. I'm sure Captain Midnight never had a more enthusiastic group in his air force. We went beyond the prerequisites required for membership. We swore secret oaths, vowing to defend women and children (men could fend for themselves) and to generally stand up for good and fight all evil.

To our chagrin, we learned that our small western Kentucky community was not crawling with Nazi saboteurs and spies. (Our leaders were constantly alerting us to be on the lookout for "fifth columnists," a term used to designate people who acted subversively out of sympathy with the enemy.)

We were not to be deterred, however, in our crusade to uncover enemies of the state. As is generally the case with fanatics, we felt that there were serpents among us, and that it was our patriotic duty to dig them out. We decided to call a meeting to discuss possible subversives in our district.

The meeting was held in the gym on Friday evening after school. As squadron commander, I had the distinction of calling the meeting to order. "Do any of you know someone who might bear watching?" I asked.

Howard Gilmore's name was brought to the floor. "I hear he's been going 'round to all the stores, buying up a lot of sugar," Les Taylor observed. "Do you think he might be operating a black market?" After due process of democratic debate, Gilmore was exonerated on the grounds that he was the local moonshiner and was producing a commodity that was in demand.

There were some disturbing reports that Mack Wilson had been going around making disparaging remarks about "dang soldiers." Of course, everyone agreed that poor half-witted Mack didn't really know what he was saying, so these reports were shelved.

It looked as if the meeting would be adjourned without finding someone worthy of

investigation until Tommy Osborn, one of the flight commanders, came up with a name. "How about old Josie Pace?" he suggested.

Josie Pace! Now there was a prime candidate. Every neighborhood seems to have its quintessential antisocial grouch, and she certainly fit this mold. Of course, Josie's worst crime was that she was a nonconformist. She didn't attend community functions, she didn't visit, and she refused to give out treats on Halloween.

Josie had never married. She lived alone on a farm inherited from her family. She subsisted mostly on what she could raise on the farm. Josie was getting on in years and didn't do a very good job of maintaining her place, so her livestock frequently got loose to forage in neighboring fields. This served to increase ill feelings toward her. So it was decided that since the next day was Saturday, we would "fly a mission" to reconnoiter the Pace farm.

We were not to be deterred in our crusade to uncover enemies of the state.

The next morning at 10 on the nose, we mustered in front of the gym. As we marched out of town wearing our aviator caps and whatever military accoutrements we could find, we felt like the Grand Army on parade.

The Pace farm was about three miles out of town. As we neared our objective, our zeal diminished. With our imaginations running amok, we could envision Nazi storm troopers doing close-order drills around the farm. One boy suddenly remembered some chores he had neglected, and others began to remember pressing matters at home.

By the time we reached the farm, I was ready to call it "mission accomplished" and return to base. I gave the welcome order, and we started the trek homeward. Then, suddenly, Josie stepped out of a clump of bushes at the side of the road!

She was hardly the threat we had conjured up. She wore a pair of overalls and a tattered chambray shirt. She looked tired, and she had obviously been crying. She tried to glare at us, but she looked more miserable than threatening.

"I recon ye're having fun, air ye?" she said, choking back a sob.

Our feelings of fear and antipathy toward Josie quickly turned to compassion, and it didn't take long to find out the source of her distress. During the night, some pranksters had taken her gate off its hinges and let her cows out. She had spent the morning trying unsuccessfully to round them up. With no one to help her, she had quickly reached her limits of endurance.

Now the Secret Squadron had a mission it could really get enthused over. We set aside our aspirations to become aviators temporarily and became cowboys. It was roundup time. In less than an hour, we had the runaway herd corralled and secured. I was ready to give the order to return to base when Josie came up with a surprise of her own.

"Now, you boys don't need to be in a hurry," she said. "I got hot vittles on the stove, and I know you must be hungry after all that chasing."

What had started as a spy mission ended up as a feast fit for a king. Josie hadn't originally planned a meal for a dozen healthy boys, but her larder was well stocked. She served us scrambled eggs, pork sausage, hot biscuits and peach preserves washed down with rivers of buttermilk.

And as one boy pointed out later, we did accomplish our mission. We got rid of an enemy—by turning her into a friend. ❖

Captain Midnight's fame moved from radio to the movie screen, as evidenced by this movie poster from 1942. Image courtesy House of White Birches nostalgia archives.

JOHN FALTER

The Wonders of TV

Chapter Three

*I*t was late afternoon, and a stagecoach was being robbed on the high plains. The marshal was pinned down behind an abutment of rocks, with the bandit blazing bullets at every movement. The lawman distracted the robber by raising his hat above the crest of the bluff, while warily sneaking his six-shooter unseen around the edge of the rocks.

Bang! Bang! Bang!

Our son shot the bad guy, saved the stagecoach from imminent danger, and good won out over evil again. He could have won the heart of the damsel in distress, but he just didn't care too much about girls in those days. All of this happened while I peacefully rested on the living room couch.

Such were the battles waged after the little screen found its way into our living rooms and our hearts. Whether he was riding with Roy Rogers and Dale Evans, catching horse thieves and cattle rustlers with the Lone Ranger, flying "out of the blue of the Western sky" with Sky King, or just hanging around the apartment with Lucy and Ricky, our little boy never realized how much the living room had changed since his mother and I were his age.

Ah, the wonder of the television era! It engendered the snack tray and the TV dinner. Televisions were moved into the kitchen so the family could watch *The Honeymooners*. Later many families abandoned all pretense about eating around the traditional supper table; they simply moved to the easy chair and the couch.

The centerpiece of the modern living room *had* to be the television. The old Philco radio was no longer the focal point that it had been for most American families in the 1930s and 1940s.

Now the family gathered around the television after supper, reveling in the new technology even when the picture was snowy and the programming was limited. Why, looking at the TV station's test pattern was better than no TV at all! Just ask our son.

In this chapter we'll remember that miracle of modern times that made our lives more entertaining. The wonders of TV were what made riding the airwaves so much more exciting back in the Good Old Days.

—*Ken Tate*

Stars are Made, not Born

...and the

Best motor oil

is <u>Made</u>, not Born

Keeping wear out of today's high-speed engines proved too big a job for the best oil nature could produce.

A better motor oil had to be built, and Texaco engineers built it — they took nature's finest crude oil, developed the best motor oil superior refining could produce, then *made it better* by means of a Balanced-Additive formula.

Advanced Custom-Made Havoline is a motor oil so much tougher, so advanced in anti-wear qualities that it actually *wear-proofs your engine for the life of your car.*

You get and keep new-engine liveliness, more power, more gasoline mileage because your motor stays cleaner. It helps prevent the formation of carbon, varnish, sludge and corrosion. Get *Advanced Custom-Made Havoline* from your Texaco Dealer, *the best friend your car has ever had.*

Wear-proofs
your
engine
for the life
of your car

Advanced
CUSTOM-MADE

HAVOLINE
MOTOR OIL
EXTRA HEAVY DUTY

TEXACO

TEXACO DEALERS
IN ALL 48 STATES

Texaco Products are also distributed in Canada and in Latin A[merica]

THE TEXAS [COMPANY]

Early TV Times

By Walt Starkey

When my bride of four months and I moved to Los Angeles in June 1948, the bandwagon of the new television industry was under way and picking up noticeable momentum. I often noticed clusters of people who had stopped to gaze at sets operating behind department store windows, seemingly enthralled by this new entertainment marvel.

The first family to acquire a TV set in our neighborhood invited us and other friends over to watch favorite programs, whetting our appetites for a set of our own. I assumed that this was happening in many neighborhoods, further accelerating TV sales.

Excited by the opportunities promised by the snowballing industry, I landed a job as one of four TV installation and servicemen for a television distributor. The understanding was that I would work part-time after I enrolled in college under the GI Bill in September.

The hypnotic appeal of television was so compelling that almost any program seemed worth watching.

I had just finished a hitch as an electronics technician in the Navy, servicing shipboard radar, sonar, electronic warfare and communications equipment, so my transition to servicing TVs was a natural one.

Troubleshooting a television set was often straightforward enough to permit me to repair the set in the customer's home. Eight out of ten problems were caused by the failure of a vacuum tube, and the symptoms the customer reported usually let me narrow the possibilities to a limited number of tubes that might be the culprit. If I had brought the correct replacement tube with me on the service call, my speedy, on-the-spot repair always seemed to impress the customer.

Other problems, however, were not so easy to deal with. The array of tools, test equipment and replacement parts I could carry with me was limited, so it was sometimes necessary to take the set back to the shop to repair it, leaving a customer who remained disgruntled until I could return his set.

My fellow servicemen were fond of swapping humorous anecdotes—often fictional, I suspected—about their experiences with customers. My friend Howard passed along one that was almost certainly fictional. It concerned a customer who was convinced that the "fizz" heard during Alka Seltzer commercials was the sound of a short circuit in his set.

Another friend, Rudy, passed along an anecdote that had the ring of truth. It concerned an angry customer who insisted the serviceman should have replaced his television set with a new one instead of just replacing the defective component. "If any part of the product I sell is bad," the customer said, "I replace the whole thing, no questions asked.

"What business are you in, sir?" Rudy asked.

"I'm a turkey wholesaler!" was the reply.

At first I was a little nervous about the rooftop work required for television installations. My nerves settled quickly, however, since California's temperate climate encourages gently sloping roofs rather than steep ones.

Installing the antenna required teamwork between me and another serviceman, or between me and the customer himself. Sometimes a third person was needed to relay the shouts we had to exchange after I climbed up to the roof with the

antenna assembly. The customer or serviceman monitored picture quality while I maneuvered the antenna from spot to spot on the roof. The objective was to maximize picture sharpness and minimize "snow" and "ghosts." (Snow was a grainy whiteness that partially obscured the picture. Ghosts were double images caused by undesired reflections of the signal from nearby buildings or terrain features.) When we found the optimum location and orientation of the antenna, I mounted and guyed it there, and my rooftop work was done.

In some areas of the city, reception was so good that an indoor "rabbit ears" antenna provided excellent picture quality, and no rooftop work was required.

My final installation chore was to coach

the customer in the use of the set's front-panel controls. Unlike today's TV sets, which demand little of the user but punching buttons on a remote control, early sets incorporated a fair number of controls—volume, focus, brightness, contrast, vertical linearity, vertical hold and horizontal hold—and they had to be used fairly frequently.

The use of volume and focus controls was obvious. Brightness and contrast could be adjusted for viewing comfort as ambient lighting conditions changed. Vertical linearity adjustment corrected for long, skinny or squat, fat images. Vertical- and horizontal-hold adjustments were needed to keep the picture from rolling drunkenly or tearing itself apart until it looked like black-and-white abstract art.

My job with the distributor enabled my wife and me to buy a 10-inch set at less than the retail price of a 7-inch set. As the months went by, I upgraded first to a 12-inch set, next a 14-inch and finally a 17-inch screen.

Los Angeles had seven VHF (very high frequency) stations at the time, none of which offered 24-hour programming. Typically, programs were transmitted from midday to 11 p.m. or midnight. As a courtesy to viewers, some stations transmitted a precise circular test pattern during nonprogram hours. This pattern helped me adjust the linearity and sharpen the focus of the picture on our set and on customers' sets after I had repaired them.

The hypnotic appeal of television was so compelling that any program seemed worth watching. My wife and I enjoyed the quiet humor of Alan Young, the zany antics of Pinky Lee, the wild slapstick of Milton Berle, the comedic genius of Jonathan Winters and the hilarious *Crusader Rabbit* cartoon series.

Spade Cooley, Merle Travis and the Collins Kids brought us the stirring beat of country music. Pat Boone, Perry Como and Dinah Shore crooned to us. Disc jockeys Al Jarvis on his *Make Believe Ballroom* and Peter Potter on his *Platter Parade* played and critiqued the latest pop-music records for us.

We were caught up in the *Space Patrol* series and *Lost in Space*; these had brief runs, but they offered little of the technological intrigue that later distinguished their descendant, *Star Trek*.

We picked our favorites among the hopefuls who sought discovery on Ted Mack's *Amateur Hour*.

For a while, professional wrestling dominated the sports scene. Of the three channels that televised local matches, my wife and I preferred Channel 5, KTLA. I can still hear announcer Dick Lane yelling "Whoa Nellie!" or "Katie bar the door!" when the action got hot. The fact that we knew that the televised mayhem was mainly showmanship didn't dilute the pleasure we took in denouncing the homicidal villainy of Gorgeous George, Baron Leone ("the Brute of Abruzzi"), and Mister Moto, and in empathizing with the heroics of Enrique Torres ("*La Pantera Negra*"), Farmer Jones and the incredibly athletic Antonino Argentine Rocca.

An indelible memory is the television coverage of the attempt to rescue 3-year-old Kathy Fiscus. On a Friday afternoon in early April 1949, the child fell into an open dry-well shaft in San Marino, Calif., plummeting 100 feet to the bottom. Her frightened cries were heard shortly after the fall, raising the hope that rescue was possible. An attempt was quickly mounted under the direction of mining and construction experts. Digging and drilling equipment were rushed to the scene, as were a number of volunteer workers. A mobile television unit, including cameras and floodlights, arrived almost as quickly, and the rescue effort was televised without interruption until its conclusion on Sunday night.

Fearing that an attempt to reach Kathy through the well shaft itself might cause a cave-in, the workers spent agonizingly long hours digging a parallel shaft so that they could tunnel to the trapped child horizontally. Like thousands of others, my wife and I spent most of the weekend riveted to our TV set until Sunday night brought a tragic end to the rescue effort. When Kathy was found dead, our hearts ached for her parents and family.

In retrospect, I believe this event was a clear indication of how much smaller our world was becoming with the advent of home television. This shrinkage has continued as technology has perfected network televising and satellite transmissions. Advances such as color television have increased our viewing pleasure, but nothing has rivaled the excitement of being on the scene when the era of home television was born. ❖

Advice in Time

By Bob Griggs

Richard M. Nixon and John F. Kennedy were running neck and neck for president of the United States in the autumn of 1960. I was working as floor director and set designer at KOIN-TV in Portland, Ore. The Kennedy campaign had planned four appearances for the senator: one, a large-audience affair at Portland's Civic Auditorium, and three others to be in studio at the television station.

The first two programs in the studio were the traditional things: the senator sitting behind a desk, and opposite him, another larger desk, behind which sat the three people responsible for questioning the prospective president. Both productions had about all the interest of a stranger's funeral. The question-and-answer part— well, the word *boring* springs immediately to mind.

As we were planning the third and final effort, Keith Lollis, the director, suggested that a less-formal setting might be the thing. We were able to come up with a nice-looking living-room setting with comfortable chairs, several small tables for coffee, a lamp or two, and some plants. The crew—all of us admitted Kennedy supporters—did a masterful job of lighting, and I even managed to purloin a really nice chair from one of the station exec's offices for the senator, having been clued in to his back problems.

The panel this time included Oregon's Senator Edith Green and several articulate local Democrats. Keith got good shots, and the whole thing achieved that rare event of not looking like a television show—just some nice people sitting and discussing politics.

When it was over, the senator started to leave, surrounded by his entourage. Then, noticing

Photo courtesy John F. Kennedy Library

Keith and me standing on the other side of the studio, he turned and started toward us. Pierre Salinger, JFK's press secretary, called out rather sharply, "Senator, we've got to go!"

"In a few minutes," said Kennedy.

"But we'll be late for the hot-dog affair at the school!"

At that point, Keith and I found out who was running things—and it wasn't Pierre! "I said, 'A few minutes!'" The words were very distinct; the tone, final. Pierre shut up.

The senator came over and shook our hands. Then he gave that famous smile. "I just wanted you to know how pleased I've been with how everything has been handled here. It was the best we've had in the campaign so far, and I hope you'll pass the word around. Now, what did you think about this format?"

Keith and I looked at each other in amazement. He was actually asking our opinion and waiting for our answers. We took a deep breath, and for the next five minutes or so, we gave our considered opinions: that we thought he looked more comfortable and approachable, and that if at all possible, he should continue the approach.

He listened with focused attention and said that was his feeling also. "It felt right!" he added. Then he glanced at his watch, grinned and said something about not keeping the hot dogs waiting, shook our hands again and walked briskly across to Pierre and his gang, and disappeared through the studio doors.

Keith and I looked at each other, dumbfounded. We'd been asked for advice by a U.S. senator, by the future *president*—although, of course, we couldn't know that then. We were, as the Brits say, "gobsmacked." That will always remain in my mind as an incredible day! ❖

Our Admiral After-School Surprise

By Danny McGuire as told to Donna McGuire Tanner

It was the winter of 1953 in the small community of Weirwood, W.Va. I was 7 years old, and my younger sister Donna was 4. My best friend, Richard, lived in the house on the right side of our home, and his aunt and uncle lived on the left side.

One day, Richard invited Donna and me to go with him to his aunt and uncle's house. He wanted to show us something. The three of us found seats on the floor, right in front of the most amazing thing we had ever seen. It was a black-and-white television set.

For a while, we watched a test pattern, and then a program called *Circle 3 Ranch* came on. It showed cowboy movies. After that came *Howdy Doody*. We soon learned that when the host asked, "Say, kids! What time is it?" we were to shout, "It's Howdy Doody time!" Other than that loud outburst, we were very quiet, lest we miss something on this new window to the world.

Word about the television spread around the neighborhood. More and more kids showed up to watch the programs.

Then, one evening, Richard's aunt stopped us on our way out and told us and the other children (except Richard) that we would not be allowed to come back anymore. I can almost understand it now, but at the time, Donna and I were just plain hurt.

Sadly, we told our mother and father that we

1954 Admiral ad,
House of White Birches nostalgia archives

were not allowed to watch television anymore. I saw a glimmer of something in Dad's eyes as he watched his two children mope around.

I attended the one-room Weirwood School, way up on a hill. It was not very far away, but just far enough that I could not see our house from it. After school, home was always a happy sight for me. And one day, I saw something new next to our house that made me sprint the whole way home.

I'd seen a new television antenna gleaming in the autumn sun. I knew that this could mean only one thing: We had a television!

That floor-model black-and-white Admiral set was a vision to behold. Donna, our baby sister, Brenda, and I plopped down onto a braided rug in front of the set. First we watched television snow, then the test pattern, and finally, our two programs.

Our parents did not object when all the other children joined us—even Richard. In no time at all, even the parents came to watch the evening programs.

Only now can I appreciate the sacrifice my parents made for my sister and me. Dad was a coal miner, so he bought the television and the antenna "on time" for a total of about $800. It was not paid off until the year that *Howdy Doody* went off the air.

That Admiral lasted for many years, until a color television came into our home. I have never forgotten my after-school surprise. ❖

TV Favorites

By Linda Shapero

I admit it: I'm a TV junkie. I'm not happy unless I get my usual five or six episodes of *Law and Order* a week, not to mention all the on-demand movies I can cram in between those episodes. As good as those are, though, I have to admit to having a soft spot for the old television shows of the 1950s and 1960s.

The first television show that I remember watching regularly was *Ding Dong School*. It first aired in 1952 and was hosted by Miss Frances, who was actually Dr. Frances Horwich, head of the Roosevelt College's education department in Chicago, Ill. The program was a precursor to shows like *Mr. Rogers' Neighborhood* and *Sesame Street*, which came much later.

In black and white, the show always started with Miss Frances ringing a handbell and calling the children to her television class. She taught simple things that preschool and kindergarten-age children could soak up like sponges, truly inspiring a love of learning. Her lessons were simple, and she was well loved by thousands of children across the country.

> *We loved to watch Superman fight "a never-ending battle for truth, justice and the American way."*

Because I grew up in Philadelphia, I can't forget a local favorite whose television show lasted an amazing 48 years. I am referring to Chief Halftown, who started at WFIL in 1951 and whose long run ended on WPVI in 1999! The Chief was a genuine Native American, though he called himself an Indian. He presented cartoons for his viewers, but he also gave us Indian lore, performed Indian dances and even taught us some Indian words. I remember (pardon the spelling) "Easss-dah-suh-sussaway," which meant, "Let's get started."

Besides appearing on television, Chief Halftown was very visible at events in the Philadelphia area, where he was a popular local celebrity.

Another early favorite of mine was *Life of Riley*, which began as a radio show but ended up on television with William Bendix in the part of Chester A. Riley. It was the tale of a blue-collar worker (an aircraft mechanic) who lived in Los Angeles, and each episode revolved around his family—wife Peg, kids Babs and Junior—and his close friend, Gillis. It was very simple and sweet.

Do you remember *Beat the Clock* with Bud Collyer as host? This early 1950s game show that continued to air until 1961. It was created by the team of Goodson and Todman, who later gave us shows such as *Password* and *Family Feud*.

Beat the Clock was a great family show—fast-paced and lots of fun—in which families performed stunts timed against the clock to

Superman (George Reeves) collars two bad guys in an episode of The Adventures of Superman.
Photo by ABC Photo Archives/ABC, Getty Images

win money and/or prizes. It never made you want to turn it off, unlike some of today's shows that can be downright revolting.

Another great early comedy was *I Married Joan*. Joan Davis portrayed Joan Stevens, the wife of Judge Bradley Stevens, played by Jim Backus. Even though she was every bit as funny as Lucille Ball of *I Love Lucy* fame, the show followed in Lucy's shadow, and *I Married Joan* was never as popular. It lasted about three years; then Jim Backus quit the show.

Do you happen to remember the words to the theme song by Richard Mack?

I married Joan,
What a girl, what a whirl, what a life.
Oh, I married Joan,
What a mind, love is blind, what a wife!

Another "adventure" show comes to mind: *The Adventures of Superman*, starring George Reeves as Clark Kent, Jack Larson as his side-kick, Jimmy Olsen, and John Hamilton as "the chief," Perry White. Looking back, I have to admit that the special effects weren't much—he never *really* looked like he was flying—but it was a lot of fun anyway. My little brother and I loved to watch Superman fight "a never-ending battle for truth, justice and the American way."

And who could forget *The Adventures of Ozzie and Harriet*, which started its long run in 1952 and ended in 1966? I don't think I started watching it until I was 10 or so, but I loved the real family of Ozzie, Harriet, David and Ricky (later known as "Rick," when he got older and became a teen heartthrob). I was in love with him—as were millions of girls around the globe.

I especially liked this show because it portrayed an ordinary family doing ordinary things, and it gave us a chance to watch the kids grow up, just as we were doing. This had to be one of the most wholesome shows ever on television. And Rick was great to look at when he sang at the end of later shows!

I don't remember any other television show being quite as elegant as *Topper*. Cosmo Topper (Leo G. Carroll) was a stodgy banker. His two personal ghosts, Marion and George Kerby (Robert Sterling and his lovely wife, Anne Jeffreys), were the previous occupants of Topper's home. After dying in an avalanche, they felt compelled to stick around to haunt him, offering endless advice. There was even a ghost St. Bernard dog, Neil, who drank gin.

This was a very classy show, helped along by Robert Sterling and Anne Jeffreys' good looks. They made a handsome couple, especially in their evening clothes!

Later on in the 1950s came more great shows. One that comes to mind is *The Gale Storm Show*, which followed on the heels of the very successful *My Little Margie*. This was a 30-minute sitcom in which Gale Storm played a cruise director. Her best friend on the ship was ZaSu Pitts ("Nugie"), and on their travels from port to port, they met all sorts of people and had great adventures. I remember a lot of singing and dancing, which gave Ms. Storm a chance to showcase her wonderful talent. And who could forget her sunny smile?

Another very cute show that I watched each week was *Bachelor Father* with suave John Forsythe as the bachelor attorney, Bentley Gregg, who was raising his young orphaned niece, Kelly. As a teenager, Kelly's dating issues became part of the parenting equation, adding all kinds of complications for bachelor father Gregg. Peter the Chinese houseboy also added lots of laughs.

Then came the cowboys shows, which were very popular from about the mid-1950s on. Hugh O'Brien starred as Wyatt Earp, a marshal in Kansas. That show lasted for 229 episodes, wrapping up in 1961.

Have Gun, Will Travel was my favorite of all the cowboy shows. Richard Boone was Paladin, a professional gun-for-hire, and he was superb in the role. Superior to the average cowboy show, it presented a hired gun who also happened to be a West Point graduate who was well versed in Shakespeare and not afraid to use his knowledge. Well-mannered and educated, Paladin was a ruthless foe nonetheless. He also had lofty values and was picky about whom he would work for. This was indeed the thinking man's cowboy show, and it worked.

Remember the theme song? "'*Have gun, will travel'" reads the card of a man, a knight without armor in a savage land …"* That song was played at the end—not the beginning—of the show each week.

Adventures in Paradise came right near the end of the decade, when my preteen hormones were starting to kick in. Who can forget the handsome Gardner McKay, who portrayed an American Korean War veteran captaining the schooner Tiki III from island to island in the South Pacific? While McKay did not have extensive acting experience (though girls like me didn't seem to notice), the show was popular, and it lasted until 1962.

I must mention two more shows that were near the top of my favorites list. The first is *Twilight Zone*, that hauntingly strange show that ran from 1959–1964 and was hosted by Rod Serling. Great stars appeared in many episodes, including Burgess Meredith, Robert Redford, Agnes Moorehead, Art Carney, William Shatner—you get the picture.

Nightmare at 20,000 Feet, starring Shatner, is also quite memorable. It scared me half to death the first time I saw it.

To this day, I can't wait until one of the local channels airs a *Twilight Zone* marathon on one of the long holiday weekends so I can burrow into the sofa and view some of those great episodes again.

Many other shows remain clear as a bell in my mind. Some of my other favorites were *December Bride*, *The Andy Griffith Show*, *Thriller* and *Sea Hunt*.

I'm sure you have your favorites too. If you are anything like me, you know that even though today's television shows have all the special effects, the Good Old Days of television were the best. ❖

Lucy and Dish Night

By F. "Micki" Harper

Back in the summer of 1954, Monday night was the most important night of the week at our house. That was the night that CBS televised the *I Love Lucy* show. It was also "Dish Night" at the movies.

The movie theater around the corner had a gimmick to get people to go to the movies on Monday nights, which were normally slow nights at the theater. If you purchased two adult tickets, you received one place setting of a "good enough for Sunday dinner" set of dishes— for free.

The ticket stubs were also put into a drum, and during the intermission, one lucky winner would have his or her choice of either the sugar and creamer or a set of matching bowls.

The idea was a pretty good one, at least from the theater owner's viewpoint. If you came once, you would probably keep coming back every Monday until you had acquired the desired number of place settings. And if you were lucky enough to win the drawing, you eventually would have a complete set of dishes, at no cost to you.

My mother wanted those dishes *and* those extra pieces. But she also wanted to watch the *I Love Lucy* show at 9 p.m. on our brand-new 14-inch black-and-white floor-model television set. That television occupied a hallowed place in the front room of our apartment, and it was only viewed on special occasions. Mother considered *Lucy* one of those occasions, and she never missed the show.

She did, however, have a problem trying to figure out how to be in both places at the same time. To be eligible to win the drawing, she had to physically be present in the movie theater during the intermission, around 8:30 p.m. She also had to be home in front of the television shortly afterward in order to see her show.

What to do? What to do? What she did, of course, was what everyone else in the neighborhood did on Monday nights: She went to the movie house to get those darn dishes. Then she sat as close to the exit door as possible and watched the first half of whatever movie was playing on the screen—and she waited.

Most of the time, my father accompanied her on these outings, protesting loudly all the way. He said we didn't need a fancy set of dishes; the ones we already owned were just fine! But it didn't do him any good. Mother needed a second body and a second ticket, so he went.

Lucille Ball photo, House of White Birches nostalgia archives

Then, after the drawing (she never won), they headed home as fast as was humanly possible, arriving just in time to catch the opening credits of *I Love Lucy*.

My sister and I were allowed to stay up and watch the show, and all four of us laughed as the characters got into silly situations. Mom and Dad were usually out of breath from the dash home and had to wait for the commercial breaks before admiring the new place setting of the almost-complete set of dishes.

Ah, those were the days! ❖

Our First Television

By Albert F. Becker

*I*n 1950, I read somewhere that my family was part of what was euphemistically called "The American Dream." Whatever else that may have meant, my father, after working long hours at the paper mill, had managed to scrape up enough money to buy those things that were most important to an 8-year-old American boy: a ball and bat, a cap gun, and our first television set.

It was a Magnavox, as I recall, with a tiny 14-inch tube ensconced in a beautiful mahogany cabinet. The speaker hid behind cheap, golden-colored fabric in the lower portion of the cabinet.

It sounded tinny, and the picture reminded me of an April snow-storm, but it still awed a young boy who was used to sitting in a noisy movie theater.

What a neat idea, I thought, watching live, moving pictures of something being broadcast hundreds of miles away! Now I could watch "Uncle Miltie" Berle, Liberace, Lucille Ball, and "99 and $^{44}/_{100}$-per-cent–pure" Ivory Soap—all in the privacy of our own home.

> *My father began tinkering with the antenna, trying to improve the reception.*

This paragon of modern technology arrived in an ordinary cardboard box that was sternly labeled "Magnavox Premium Black & White Television: This Side UP."

The setup was tough. After we got past what seemed like 55 pounds of cardboard filler and spacers (plastic foam hadn't become the choice of packaging engineers yet), Dad still had to spend countless hours on the roof, assembling the antenna, lining up the elements just so, attaching the bracket to the peak of the roof, and then trying to attach the 300-ohm lead wire to the antenna.

Naturally, after 18 days of brilliant spring weather with no whisper of a breeze, he wound up trying to do it in near gale-force winds. For once, I couldn't bear to watch my father working on something; I knew he was going to be blown away like Dorothy in *The Wizard of Oz*.

But at last he won the day, and we finally could see something flickering on the television screen besides a dull gray background. We had no reason to think anything evil was going on behind that 14-inch tube. Yet malevolence lurked there, all right, in the form of poor reception.

My father began tinkering with the antenna, trying to improve the reception, while my mother stood in the doorway, shouting directions and encouragement.

"How's that?" Dad would holler.

"Getting better," Mom would say.

"How's that?"

"Move it a little more."

"Better?"

"Yes! It just needs a little more."

Meanwhile, the picture showed various degrees of ghosts and snow, flickering up and down, or from side to side, the sound fading in and out as the antenna desperately searched for elusive electromagnetic beams that danced in the air. Slowly it would improve; Uncle Miltie would quit leaning at a 45-degree angle and stand straight up. And then, just as our hopes soared and smiles lit our faces—*zap!* The signal would vanish.

"No, no, no!" Mama cried. "You went too far! Back it up a little!"

"Whaddya mean? *How* little?"

"I don't know. Just a little."

After a pause, from the topside we heard, "How's that?"

"A little better. Try it some more."

Dad's muffled voice would filter down again. "Is that better?"

"Yes, yes, you've almost got it—oh, no! You went too far the other way now!" Curses and unprintable epithets rained down from the roof.

Eventually, of course, he got it right, and we settled in each evening to watch our beautiful black-and-white television shows. The problem was that half the time, we couldn't figure out what shows were going to be on.

"Whaddaya wanna watch?"

"I dunno. Whadda *you* wanna watch?"

"I don't know. What's on?"

"I don't know. Flip through the channels and let's see."

Keep in mind that we had never imagined

such luxuries as remote controls, so every channel selection had to be made by bending over the television and turning the knob.

Click. Click. Click.

"Wait a minute—what's that?"

"I dunno. Some kind of game show."

"Who's in it?"

"I dunno. I don't know television stars."

"Well, let's watch this, I guess."

Fortunately, some bright wig came to America's rescue and began publishing the *TV Guide* in early 1953. This was a big help, especially when the first color programs began airing later that year. The guide indicated different kinds of programs by tiny icons next to the program names, and we deliberately tuned in to that show—whether we usually watched it or not—just to see what the icon meant.

The television became our nightly ritual, an institution. As programming increased, our horizons expanded, and our evenings were filled with comedies, mysteries, documentaries and even fairly educational shows, such as *Omnibus*. But Fridays were the best because we kids could stay up late, and evening TV was overrun with family programming. That's when we enjoyed such classics as *The Adventures of Ozzie and Harriet, The Life of Riley* with William Bendix, *Our Miss Brooks,* in which the adorable Eve Arden foreshadowed Murphy Brown, and *Mr. and Mrs. North*, a detective show starring Richard Denning and Barbara Britton.

I did encounter a bit of a problem on Thursday nights. Because of school, I had to be in bed by 10 o'clock—but one of my favorite shows, *Victory at Sea*, came on at 11:30. Occasionally, my parents, staring transfixed at the screen, forgot to make me go to bed. The old adage

"Uncle Miltie"—Milton Berle.

1951 RCA Victor television ad, House of White Birches nostalgia archives

"Silence is golden" never was more true than at those times; if I kept my mouth shut, I could get away with it about 20 percent of the time.

Other times, I had to resort to more serious measures, like tantrums. I would throw myself on my bed, sobbing and wailing piteously and loudly to make sure my parents heard.

Sometimes it worked; my parents would grimace and tell me I could get up and watch it, as long as I kept quiet. More often than not, however, I got no sympathy at all—just repeated threats of bodily harm to my backside if I didn't zip it. Knowing from experience how adept my mother and father were with a belt, a switch from an acacia bush out back, or just the flat of the hand, I generally zipped it. I wasn't the brightest kid around, but I wasn't stupid, either.

I really had little to complain about. There were plenty of programs for kids during the day and especially on Saturdays, when cartoons began flooding the programming. *Mighty Mouse* was followed swiftly by *Heckle and Jeckle* and a host of others. I loved those shows—especially the music when the mouse superhero suddenly burst on the scene to the words, "Here I come, to save the day!" Gosh, who needed Superman when you had a mouse who could do everything the Man of Steel could do—and wasn't bothered by Kryptonite?

Our idyllic TV universe suddenly came to an end early in 1953, when NBC announced rather pompously that, starting that fall, they would broadcast programs in "living color." And such programs could not be watched on black-and-white televisions without an "adapter." Boy, does *that* sound familiar?

So, in order to see the same programs in color, we would have to buy a new television set. And we had barely begun to pay *this* one off! ❖

The Impossible Scheme

By Vincent Argondezzi

*I*t has taken its place by enduring acclaim as one of the greatest football games ever played. A quick perusal of the events that took place on the football field at the Ohio State University in 1935 certainly supports this reputation. Notre Dame was outweighed, outmanned and outscored until the final seconds in a turnabout that silenced the partial Ohio State crowd.

My uncle was a Notre Dame fan, as we all were in my family, so it was with great excitement that we assembled in his living room to watch the game. (He had the only television set in the area.) That fall of 1935, we were living in Manayunk, a suburb of Philadelphia.

The television was an Atwater Kent, and the slightest movement caused the picture to blur. So my uncle announced that no one should move once the game started.

"That includes you, too, Caesar," he said, as our big cat made his appearance.

We were very subdued as the Ohio State team ran at will against Notre Dame. This didn't surprise anyone, and yet it excited that hope that was so legendary when the Irish ran onto a gridiron.

But the set sputtered and the picture faded. It looked like that would be it for our viewing Saturday. But not so. My uncle fashioned an emergency antenna from wire and handed it to me. "What's this for?" I asked. I didn't think it was an unreasonable question.

"What's it *for*?" my uncle repeated. "What's it *for*? Carry it to the kitchen roof so we can get better reception!"

"But I wanted to watch the game, Uncle."

"Jim, here is your chance to show your love for the fighting Italians. There is no picture without your help."

"That's 'Fighting Irish,' Uncle," I said.

Well, I went up to the roof and held the hanger as high as I could, staying as close to the window as I could so I could hear the announcer. Notre Dame was making a comeback—an unbelievable one—in the second half. After being demolished in the first half, Andy Pilney, the Irish quarterback, ran and passed the Irish for two touchdowns. But they missed both extra points, and then time was running out.

At this point, the picture faded again, and the sound diminished. Then I heard my uncle announce in a very loud voice, "Move to the edge of the roof and hold the aerial out more! We are going to win this game! It's fading, can you hear me? Keep moving to the right!"

That was a mistake. I made my way to the right just as Pilney threw for a touchdown. I fell off the roof when I got so excited that I forgot I didn't have any more roof left on the right!

"I am proud of you," my uncle said later. "Thanks to you holding that hanger up as you fell, I could see the Shakespeare pass that won the game."

We all do what we have to do. ❖

Television Don

By Larry Nestor

We got our first television set in October 1949. I guess Mom and Dad wondered why there was such a fuss about Milton Berle and this new "luxury" that was selling like the proverbial hotcakes. I'm sure that my brother Don and I made it known that Bob and Terry Erickson, our good buddies who lived two houses down, had a set. They even had invited me over to watch Uncle Miltie one Tuesday evening.

Here came the delivery truck from the department store. Up the stairs came our new television—a Philco 12-inch black-and-white model with a brown plastic console.

My brother, who was 4 years old when the television arrived, immediately gravitated to certain shows; *The Gabby Hayes Show*, *Kukla, Fran & Ollie* and *Garfield Goose* were among his favorites. Others were *Noontime Comics with Uncle Johnny Coons*; *The Cinnamon Bear*; *Tom Corbett, Space Cadet* and the *Our Gang* comedies.

He especially got a kick out of Gabby Hayes. His "Yer daaaarn tootin'!" and "They're shot from a gun!" regarding Quaker Puffed Wheat and Puffed Rice, brought my brother special delight, and his face beamed whenever Gabby went into those bits. Don even mimicked his voice and mannerisms; the only thing missing was the bushy gray beard.

Don would find a comfortable seat and dig in, ready for an afternoon of viewing fun, interrupted only by frequent visits to the pantry and kitchen.

Don was really susceptible to the TV commercials. If a cereal was being advertized, Don would get up, walk to the kitchen and pour a bowl of cereal, preferably the one being advertized. Then, adding milk and grabbing a tablespoon, he would return to his warm spot on the sofa. Frosted Flakes was his favorite.

If the next commercial was an ad for Bosco chocolate syrup (Frazier Thomas of *Garfield Goose* had a way of making this product sound like the greatest thing since bubble gum), he would get up, pour a tall glass of milk and then add lots of Bosco, stirring it until at least most of the chocolate syrup had dissolved.

My brother did occasionally miss some good parts to the shows as he moved back and forth between his chair and the kitchen. Sometimes he seemed to be in a hypnotic state, rarely saying anything as he left the TV and headed for the food supply. My mom and I would just shake our heads; it seemed that Don was being controlled by

It seemed that Don was being controlled by powers zoomed into our house from Chicago and New York.

powers zoomed into our house from Chicago and New York. It seemed quite funny, but in time, Mom hid certain items to make sure my brother didn't consume an inordinate amount of calories. Sometimes she would ask me to take Don's hand and walk him around so she could concentrate on the task at hand.

TV's influence on my little brother showed up every time we went grocery shopping at A&P, Kroger's or Hillman's. Don would walk along beside Mom and pick out products he'd seen on television, and then add them to our shopping cart—usually cookies, candy, cereal and fruit drinks. Mom would buy a few of the items, but most of the time, she would wait until Don's back was turned, then slyly slip them back onto their shelves. Otherwise her bill would have been way over budget.

Sometimes my mother resembled a juggler, slipping cookies and other goodies back in place as others were on the way into the cart. But I guess Don came by it honestly; our father always had a huge sweet tooth! ❖

TV Was Young and So Was I

By Mary Jo Collins

I was 16, scared, and had never seen a television studio, camera or director when I auditioned on the air for the candy commercial on the Saturday night 10 p.m. news. The father of a friend from school owned the candy store, wrote the copy and sent it with his daughter Thursday. I memorized it. But at that moment, I couldn't remember it or my name.

Mom dropped me off at Channel 5 at 8 p.m. I stood on the corner with tears rolling down the pancake makeup I hoped television people wore.

It was a long walk from the curb to the impressive station with the towering antenna. I wasn't anxious to get there.

"Can I help you, miss?"

The receptionist was a bleached blonde, skinny where she should be. She looked like a perfect candy saleslady.

"I'm here to do a commercial on tonight's news."

She dialed the phone, said something softly, and we waited. Maybe they'd forgotten … maybe it was the wrong night … maybe I could go home!

Then the chocolate bunny collapsed, and so did I. That's the way it was in the Good Old Days.

Then the door marked "Keep Out" opened. "Come right in, miss," a man said.

I followed him down the long row of closed doors to Studio B, which looked just like gym 101 at school. The concrete room had a 4-foot area lit from all directions. Two canvas walls with a sign, "Fanny Farmer," angled behind a table filled with candies. A long piece of velvet covered the boxes and stacks of books and wood chunks that propped up the display.

"Stand on the masking tape. Don't move, or you'll cover the sign or be out of the light. I'm glad you didn't wear white—causes a halo, you know."

I *didn't* know. I rejoiced in the oxford cloth blouse with the calico flower at the neck: old, comfortable and—thank heavens!—blue.

"Meet John on camera 1, Pete on 2. You ever done this before?" I shook my head no and she continued, "That's what I thought. When the red light goes on, start. The camera will move in slowly, focusing on your hands as you cut open the candy. Tape your copy to the back of the box and read. Paragraph 3 is a close-up of your face; look right into the big lens and smile Let's give it a try."

"Stand by."

"I'm your friendly Fanny Farmer sale-slady," I began voice quavering, "and I have some good news for you."

"Cut—cut, that means stop. They only sent one buttercream egg. Don't actually cut it open till we're on the air. Be sure no chocolate goes in; we'll be on an extreme close-up."

"Sure," I said. I wondered how you kept the chocolate from going in—wondering how you kept the knife from shaking.

"Good job. Go through it again if you want. Try to relax. There's coffee in the control room. Two hours to go. Do you want a boom or lavaliere? The mike, I mean—do you want to wear it or have it over your head? Give her a boom."

By 10 p.m., George Gobel had waved good-bye, the newsman tried his smile, the weather board had been decorated and a wrestler was hovering over the guest chair at the sports desk. I heard a hollow voice say, "Stand by."

I looked at the chocolate rabbit propped on five books too close to the lights. The front and back of the hollow bunny were straining to melt and meet.

"We're brought to you tonight by your good friends at Fanny Farmer."

I said to the big red eye, "I'm your friendly Fanny Farmer saleslady, and I've some good news for you." I took the knife, steadying my hand on the table. *Please, chocolate, don't crumble in on the creamy white nougat and rich yellow center.*

Camera 2 was so close I could see myself in the lens. "For your convenience, these Fanny Farmer shops will be open tomorrow." The light went off, and I read the addresses. Then the chocolate bunny collapsed, and so did I. That's the way it was in the Good Old Days.

The author (right) is amused at the antics of Phyllis Diller during a live broadcast of her television program in the 1950s. After the show they shopped for feathers for Miss Diller's act.

My next job was as a checkerboard hostess, three days a week for Ralston Purina—and still with no auditions, no competition.

The modeling schools were sending pretty young things by 1956, but they had no experience writing copy, calling camera shots or serving sponsors.

For Women Only was my daily radio show; *The Early Show With Mary Jo*, was my daily TV offering, plus a children's show, interviews and the weather.

If the Magic Marker for my weather board was missing, I always knew where to look. Harry Prisoner's kids liked to draw pictures under Daddy's desk while he read the news.

Phyllis Diller, with her electric-shock hairdo and A-frame dress, climbed onto my desk and flew off. She had just been discovered on the old Steve Allen *Tonight Show* and was in town to promote her nightclub act. We shopped for feathers for her costume after the show.

Charlton Heston flexed his cheekbones and talked about Moses and *The Ten Commandments*. Betty Friedan hailed me as the perfect example of the liberated woman and almost ruined my amateur standing.

The opening night of *Cinderama*, my first remote, imagine me interviewing Mitzi Gaynor. But Mitzi was ill, so they sent a substitute—a shy starlet with no last name, Ann-Margret.

In the Good Old Days, I flew to Hollywood to appear in Chuck Connors' *Rifleman* as a publicity promotion. For three days, I was due at the studio at 7 a.m. for makeup, costumes, rehearsal. "More apple pie, sir?" was my line.

Chuck Connors said, "No thanks," but we made the cover of *TV Guide*.

We broadcast daily from the Minnesota State Fair where I was charmed by an orangutan, felt the milk vein of a golden Guernsey and became an expert on the kazoo.

We worked Christmas Day and New Year's Eve. It was all live in 1959. Now there are videotape and minicams and meteorologists, idea girls, copywriters, producers. But they can't have more fun than we did in the 1950s, when TV was young and so was I. ❖

Not on My Roof

By Louise Bartholomew

Above the treetops in our neighborhood, one lone antenna lingers. But not so long ago, one would have thought that our world was a pincushion held in place by antennas! When I think back to the beginning of television, I don't recall Milton or Lucy, but rather the sprouting antennas that announced to all that the occupants had a television.

Perhaps this is such a vivid memory because the one that sprouted from our house was completely unexpected. My daughter and I were coming home from shopping, and as we stepped off the bus, we stopped for a moment to admire our new roof.

Then we did a double take; something new had been added. Yes, there was an antenna on our roof! We had never discussed purchasing a television, since our budget simply wouldn't bend that far. And now this! Well, it called for an explanation.

I found my husband, Elmer, inside, sputtering and spewing into the telephone, his face getting redder by the second. "No, absolutely not!" he declared. Then he slammed the phone down.

"What's going on?" I asked.

"Didn't you see it?" he inquired. "They tramped around all over the new roof in this hot weather and put a blasted antenna up there! Now they want to take it down! We didn't order it—Gibsons did!"

I remembered that Gloria Gibson, our next-door neighbor, had mentioned that they had been thinking about buying a television.

When Elmer adamantly refused to let anyone do further damage to the roof by removing the antenna, we ended up buying it for half-price. It was some time before we could put it to use. In the meantime, it was difficult to explain. How could we have an antenna but no television? ❖

The Spelling Bee

By Birney Dibble

A spelling bee for adults? On prime-time television? That's *just* what it was, in 1951, back in the early days of television in Chicago. How exciting! Programmers in those days were desperate for almost anything to fill empty time slots, even during the evening hours. They ran cartoons and old movies. They tried to turn favorite radio programs into television programs, with limited success.

And for about six months, they aired a weekly, hour-long spelling bee beginning at 8 p.m.—on Wednesdays, I believe. They pitted teachers against their students, bosses against their secretaries, civil engineers against electrical engineers, parents against their kids, and many other combinations I can't remember.

I do remember the time they pitted five Cook County Hospital interns against five student nurses. I was an intern at the time and was one of the five invited to participate. Only medical terms would be used. The interns would clearly have the advantage—right?

The moderator pronounced the word. Each of us wrote it on a card and passed it to him. The correct answers were tallied against the misspelled responses.

The moderator started out with easy ones to warm us up: "biliary" … "placenta" … "cerebrospinal" … "gluteus."

Then the words got harder: "islet of Langerhans" … "latissimus dorsi" … "shigella" … "Ménière's syndrome" … "Schwabach's test."

Then it got really tough: "tripanosomiasis" … "gnothostoma spinigirim" … "pneumoconiosis" … "pseudocryptorchidism."

The girls stayed right in there with us. Toward the end of the hour, we were tied, believe it or not.

But then the moderator hit us with the toughest one of all: "leptospirosis icterohaemorrhagica." All of us interns spelled it without the *e* in the middle of the word. One of the nurses spelled it with the *e*.

They won! Each of them received a portable radio, a real prize in those days when most radios still had huge vacuum tubes and were distinctly *not* portable.

We interns each received a Pepsi Cola cooler, which was very nice because buying one was beyond the means of most of us on a salary of $15 a month.

I used that cooler for many years, until it was stolen one night. It was filled with fillets of walleye and northern pike, and it was sitting outside in a Fergus Falls, Minn., park while my wife and I were sleeping in our car. ❖

"Sportster"

PHILCO 675

"Knockabout"

PHILCO 672

"Rancher"

PHILCO 670

Matches Lighting Up the Screen

By Jess Hernandez

The year 1947 was notable because it was a milestone in the advent of television. Shortly thereafter, millions of TV antennas perched atop hotels, restaurants and homes. That year was exceptional to me personally as well, because I, along with the whole family, was exposed to wrestling on the TV. Wednesday night at our home was reserved for broadcasts of the grunt-and-groan sport from the Olympic Auditorium in Los Angeles.

What made the TV wrestling shows funny and interesting were the colorful descriptions and announcing of Dick Lane. On many an evening, Lane would find himself about to be clobbered on the head by a monstrous madman who had put a hood over his face. Hiding his face behind a mask just added to the fun and merriment. Sometimes the family would argue as to whether the matches were for real, considering all the blood and mayhem inside the ring.

Do you recall some of the superstar heroes of 1947, the first big year of national TV coverage? At the Olympic Wrestling Club, the meanies and good guys included Argentina Rocca, Gorgeous George, Wild Red Berry, Danny McShain, Great Togo, the Swedish Angel and Baron Michele Leone.

I liked Count Billy Varga. Varga wore a colorful championship belt every time he got inside the ring. His father, Joe Varga, was a bona fide count, and he won three

The outrageous Gorgeous George.

amateur world titles in the same evening. If you don't believe that, it's in *Ripley's Believe It of Not.*

Bill Varga not only won the world's championship, but after he retired from the sport, he became an actor and appeared with Rita Hayworth on *The Munsters* TV show and was in the movies *The Lemon Drop Kid* and *Pier 23.*

Anyone who's a wrestling fan remembers Gorgeous George. He draped himself in an elegant robe and styled his hair in a wave. He loved to sprinkle perfume over himself *and* his opponents.

Then there was Lord Carlton, who didn't climb through the ropes unless he was decked out in his long, flowing cape and monocle, and was closely followed by his faithful valet.

Another colorful wrestler was Baron Michele Leone, who loved to build up his goodwill with the fans by flipping lollipops to the kids!

On occasion, the fans were just as outrageous and colorful as the contestants. Many times, some female fan at ringside stuck a hat pin into a wrestler who had been thrown outside the ring. Some fans even threw bottles at helpless wrestlers. In San Diego, Calif., fans started a fire when a guy got out of control and hit the referee and some spectators.

Of course, watching the matches on TV, we didn't worry about violence inside or outside the ring. Everybody at the house seemed happy and relaxed as we watched wrestling on TV in the 1940s and early 1950s. It was better than going to the movies.

But after Gorgeous George retired, along with Argentina Rocca and Billy Varga, I lost interest in wrestling. The worst part came when colorful Dick Lane, the man responsible for making the sport popular in Los Angeles, left KTLA Channel 5 and retired.

Today, wrestling on TV seems so outdated and gruesome. The fans are mostly violent and aggressive. Nobody laughs anymore or seems to enjoy the matches.

To me, the happiest days and fun times were the late 1940s, when comedy was king at the Olympic Auditorium. The Good Old Days will never return—and that's bad for wrestling fans like me. ❖

The Big Event

By Frank Houlihan

It was 1947, and television was catching on in my Bronx, N.Y., neighborhood. One of our first neighbors to own a TV asked Dad if we'd like to see the upcoming light heavyweight championship fight on TV. Melio Bettina and Gus Lesnevich would battle for the title at Madison Square Garden.

On May 23, my dad and I ambled up to our neighbor's apartment, and were seated in the living room with other neighbors. Our host passed out sodas and pretzels.

It was getting close to fight time, and the ring announcer started to introduce other fighters from the audience. The two contestants had entered the ring earlier and were now waiting for the introductions to end.

The two boxers were called to the center of the ring by the referee, Bill Cavanaugh, who explained the New York state rules to both boxers. They returned to their corners, and everyone waited eagerly for the bell signaling the start of round 1.

As the bell rang, I headed for the bathroom. Mother Nature wouldn't wait. Returning to the living room, I noticed that everyone was somber, and the fighters were sitting on their stools in their corners.

"What happened?" I asked. "Didn't the fight start yet?"

"The fight's over," Dad said. "Lesnevich won by a knockout, knocking Bettina down three times." I'd missed the whole thing!

That fight set a Madison Square Garden record for the fastest knockout ever recorded, at 59 seconds of the first round.

Dad thanked the host for the invite. Then we left and walked home. Well, at least I had enjoyed some soda and a few pretzels.

After that, other neighborhood families began to purchase TVs. Wednesday night fights were a big hit, but even after all these years, I still remember the fight I didn't see. ❖

Captain Video

By Gary Mielo

*M*any modern media heroes for children represent the sad axiom that "Might makes right." Recent pop culture figures teach our children that violence is the acceptable vehicle for settling disputes. The subtler expressions of cunning and shrewdness have been rendered obsolete.

When I met Captain Video, one of television's original science-fiction heroes, I didn't need a demonstration of his virtues. Like any hero-worshiping 10-year-old in the mid-1950s, I assumed they implicitly existed. Nevertheless, on this day, I was lucky enough to experience firsthand the Captain's cleverness and loyalty. And the lesson has stayed with me for all these years.

Al Hodge as Captain Video

I was with my father in the studio audience of a local New York TV station, watching technicians, directors and producers prepare for another broadcast of a weekend kid's show called *Wonderama.* The show featured a number of fading television personalities. Al Hodge, the renowned Captain Video, was one of them.

Formerly radio's Green Hornet, Hodge played Captain Video for the DuMont Network in the early 1950s. During the show's run of nearly six years, the Captain was portrayed as a scientific genius who was the "master of time and space, and guardian of the safety of the world." Integrity and fairness were the prime components of the Captain's persona.

Anxious to get a memento from so formidable a figure, I had come equipped with a fountain pen and a leather-bound autograph book. These items within reach, I kept a vigil for the Captain from my seat.

When I spotted Hodge coming onto the set, I immediately got up, and with book outstretched, closed in on him. I asked for an autograph. He smiled modestly, and after asking my name, wrote "to Gary, Best Wishes, Al Hodge, Captain Video."

As he handed the book back to me, I praised his exploits fighting the nefarious Dr. Pauli, his archenemy. A proud smile spread across his face. I followed this with a casual mention of the Galaxy, one of the hottest rocket ships under his command. "You remember that?" he asked with mild incredulity. I nodded yes. His face brightened momentarily. Then one of the production assistants called him away. I went back to my seat, flush with accomplishment.

About 20 minutes later, the Captain came back onto the set. This time he was accompanied by someone touting an official-looking clipboard. They wanted eight kids to be on the Captain's quiz show, a segment scheduled for that afternoon. I edged my aisle seat out a little farther, hoping to be noticed. I was. The Captain saw me and asked if I wanted to be one of his rangers. I looked over at my father, who nodded.

The setup was simple. We eight lucky kids were divided into Rocket Ship Teams A and B. We were shown a short film, and then we were asked questions about it. The stakes were high: an elaborate, wood-boxed chemistry lab would go to the winners, while a flimsy plastic space helmet would be awarded to the losers. I wanted that chemistry set—not because I had a scientific bent, but because it meant I was one of the Captain's winners.

Unfortunately, my team lost. As soon as the show went off, we were given our prizes and handshakes from the Captain. The plastic helmet was mine. I was just about to go back to my seat when a kid from the winning team came up to the Captain. He didn't want the chemistry set; he wanted the helmet instead.

Instantly, three voices from Rocket Ship A joined mine: "I'll trade!" The Captain stepped in, quelling the shouts. He put his hand on my shoulder and stated emphatically, "This boy said it first." No one disputed his judgment.

A satisfied smile appeared on the Captain's face. I knew he was glad I had gotten the chemistry set, even if by default. I might have lost the quiz, but I came up with first prize anyway. Something like that could only happen with the intervention of Captain Video.

More than 20 years elapsed before I heard about Al Hodge again. After *Wonderama*, his obscurity was total. Then, one day, a friend gave me an obituary torn from a newspaper. I immediately recognized the postage-stamp–size picture of Hodge. The article, written from a UPI bulletin, told how he had died "alone and almost forgotten."

Alone and forgotten—two fates worse than death. But he *wasn't* forgotten. I have thought and talked about my meeting with Hodge dozens of times during my adult years. His sly smile outlasted the prize he won for me. It has lingered all through the intervening years.

Captain Video might have died alone—but aren't captains trained for that? ❖

Super Circus

By Hazel Gray Miller

In January 1949, *Super Circus* first aired on TV, originating from the Civic Theater in Chicago on the ABC network. The live show was televised until June 1956.

Sunday evenings, our family gathered in front of our black-and-white television set to watch *Super Circus*. When a clown blew a whistle, the show began.

Mary Hartline, a beautiful blonde in a short majorette costume and boots, ran across the stage with the clowns and directed the *Super Circus* band with her baton.

The handsome, dark-haired ringmaster, Claude Kirchner, announced acrobatic and animal acts before a live television audience. I held my breath with the lion tamers. Could those big cats get loose? Huge elephants paraded on the stage or stood on their heads. Small dogs jumped through hoops.

Nicky the Tramp and Cliffy the Clown threw pies at each other. Scampy the Boy Clown sometimes joined in; he always had Mary Hartline helping him out of trouble.

One of the favorite spots for children in the audience was the Penny Dip Bowl, where kids filled their hands with as many pennies as they could hold.

As we watched the show, my dad and brother appreciated Mary Hartline's beauty. My sister, who also twirled a baton, enjoyed her leading the band and twirling. My mother and I liked the animal acts, and I confess to swooning over Claude Kirchner.

Super Circus spawned a number of toys that were sold during the show's tenure. There were Mary Hartline dolls, paper-doll coloring books, a *Little Golden Book of Super Circus* and a hand puppet of Mary. All of these are now collectibles, especially sought by those of us who remember thrilling to the acts of *Super Circus* on their TV sets back in the Good Old Days. ❖

For Better or Worse

By Bob Cusack

"You've come a long way, baby." But have you really? In these days of cable television, don't you marvel at the number of available channels? Yet, how many times have you stared at TV listings and found yourself saying, "There's nothing on tonight"? The quantity may be there—but what has happened to the quality? When television was in its commercial infancy in the late 1940s, we had very few channels to watch.

Yet, we watched. Granted, we were captivated by its novelty. Still, it was pure entertainment all the way. We didn't need a "lock box" to control who saw what program. It was all for the family. And no one complained, whether they were 6 or 60.

My first recollection of television was seeing a small black-and-white screen in the window of a department store. I had to walk by that store to get home from school. It became a ritual to stop and glare at that strange device with pictures too nervous to stand still.

Sure, there were glitches and imperfections. But didn't that make it more fun?

Most of the time, cartoons were all there were to be seen. Yet, there would always be a crowd, three and four deep, mesmerized by it all. They watched. And they watched. My arrival home was often delayed.

Few people could afford a television set in those days. A console cost about $500. So we'd do the next best thing—become friendly with a neighbor who had a set or a family member who might be better off. In our case, it was a little of each. Most of the time, we visited aunts Della and Gertrude, and their oval-screen Philco, usually on Tuesday or Sunday nights.

Tuesday was Uncle Miltie night on the *Texaco Star Theater*. Uncle Miltie was Milton Berle. He was Mister Television. It began with a jingle sung by a quartet dressed in service-station uniforms. "Oh, we're the men from Texaco. We go from Maine to Mexico. …"

Miltie was a master of slapstick. He wore silly costumes, and he was always onstage. No matter who was performing, Miltie had to get into the act! But he must have done something right; his show ran from 1948 until 1956.

On Sunday, it was Ed Sullivan. Originally his show was called *Toast of the Town*. Ed was a poker-faced columnist who acted as host on the variety show. His guests ranged from Russian gymnasts to the current rage in pop singers like Elvis and Ricky Nelson. His show marked the first American television appearance of The Beatles.

Ed insisted on strict censorship, however. That meant that "Elvis the

The Ed Sullivan Show *featuring The Beatles went on the air on Sunday, Feb. 9, 1964, from CBS's studio in New York City. Ed Sullivan is pictured at far left; band members (from left), Paul McCartney, George Harrison, John Lennon and drummer Ringo Starr. Photo by CBS Photo Archive, Getty Images*

Pelvis" could only be shown from the waist up. Sullivan said Presley's gyrations were just too suggestive. Ed was not a smooth emcee, but he knew which guests would get people to tune in.

Impressionists had a field day with Ed— "Right heeere on our stage." Sullivan was amused by it all. *The Ed Sullivan Show* was the longest-running variety show in industry history. It was seen from 1948 to 1971.

Our first TV set was a Stromberg-Carlson. It had a green eye we would close for fine tuning. I can remember waiting for television to sign on at 5:30 in the evening! We would rush through supper and often begin by watching a

test pattern before Howdy Doody appeared.

That's right, Howdy Doody! In those days, we would watch anything and everything, even if it was a children's program. We were couch potatoes before the expression ever existed.

We would be entranced by that 12-inch screen right into the night, even though sign-off came early. There was no daytime or late-night viewing back then.

What was a typical night like on TV in 1950? First came *Howdy Doody* with Buffalo Bob, Clarabell the Clown and Mayor Bluster.

Fifteen-minute variety shows starring singers Roberta Quinlan and Irish tenor Morton

Buffalo Bob Smith and his sidekick, Howdy Doody, pictured before an episode of The Howdy Doody Show. *Photo courtesy House of White Birches nostalgia archives.*

Downey preceded John Cameron Swayze and his equally short network newscast.

Swayze would greet us with "And a good evening to you" and close with "Glad we could get together." I can still hear him "hopscotching the world for headlines." Swayze was more of a newsreader than a reporter, but his precise diction and natty appearance made him instantly recognizable.

Prime time after 7 p.m. consisted of programs like *Philco Television Playhouse*, *The Goldbergs*, *Studio One* and *Ford Theater*. Sunday nights at 9 we'd see *The Fred Waring Show*, usually including choral versions of old standards.

This was followed by *Garroway at Large*. Dave Garroway was more of a host who tied things together. The show had a few singers who did the latest pop tunes, and it also included a few innovative gimmicks.

Those of us fortunate enough to have seen television develop before our very eyes can also look back with amusement at its growing pains. Do remember, this was before the days of video editing. It was live and happening, right then and there! Sure, there were glitches and imperfections that would certainly be unacceptable by today's standards. But didn't that make it more fun?

I can recall one show, either *Studio One* or *Playhouse 90*, during which the camera was following the main actor into a hotel hallway. As the camera trailed the actor to his room, the actor opened the door. That camera got a full view of another camera inside the room. I guess you have to make mistakes to learn from them.

Then there was a detective show called *Man Against Crime* starring Ralph Bellamy in the original lead as a New York City private eye who didn't use a gun! Imagine that today! It was sponsored by a tobacco company. Its opening format made it prone to error. Live, while the theme song was heard, viewers would see a silhouette of the main character smoking a pipe. One night, he choked! I wonder how the sponsor explained that?

When it came to Westerns, we had our share. *Gunsmoke* had enough staying power to hang on for 20 years, from 1955 to 1975. Marshal Dillon, Doc, Chester, Festus and Miss Kitty kept us coming back week after week.

Bonanza came in second to *Gunsmoke* among long-running Westerns. Lorne Green, Pernell Roberts, Dan Blocker and Michael Landon made a living on the Ponderosa Ranch from 1959 to 1973, although Roberts left for greener pastures in 1965.

And did we ever have sitcoms! *The adventures of Ozzie and Harriet* was the longest running, telecast from 1952 to 1966—and that was preceded by a long run on radio. Little Ricky and David grew up right before our eyes!

Other comedies with considerable success included *The Jack Benny Show*, *I Love Lucy* and *The Dick Van Dyke Show*. No one was ever offended. All we did was get sore ribs from laughing!

Others entertained us in gracious style. Perry Como first showed up on a regular basis in 1948 with a variety show that ran until 1966. After that, he appeared periodically on specials.

Red Skelton amused us with his own special style of humor for 20 years. He developed his own characters back in vaudeville and in radio, and took them with him to TV. Skelton, an inveterate ad-libber, delighted in breaking up his guest stars. In doing so, he brought even more laughter into our homes.

For many, it's hard to picture life without television. Unfortunately, today's television lacks that wholesome quality that was so much a part of those early efforts. Technically we certainly are a lot better off. There's no argument in that regard.

However, escapism has been replaced by too much realism. It's too graphic and violent! And with so many new channels turning up on cable, it's becoming worse!

The industry has come a long way, but to what avail? While I am not saying eliminate the new and bring back the old, I am saying, let's clean up our act.

Today's technology coupled with yesterday's values just might make you feel good about what you watch. ❖

American comedian and actor Red Skelton appears as Freddie the Freeloader, a recurring character from The Red Skelton Show *in the 1960s. Photo by CBS Photo Archive, Getty Images*

Being First at Something

By Jeanne Knape

"Mom, come look! Dad's got another radio," announced my younger sister as she let the screen door slam behind her. Mom ran to the porch. When she saw her husband carrying the mentioned item, she pursed her lips. She had told him several times that our family didn't need any more radios. Three in any family was two too many.

As the screen door slammed one more time, Dad appeared, grinning like the Cheshire cat from *Alice in Wonderland*. He set the newest mechanical addition on the hall table.

"Dan, how dare you bring …" But she didn't get to finish her protest because Dad threw his arms around her, giving her a hug.

"Just think, Doris, we're the *first* at something!" he said.

"Yes, the first family in this town to own too many radios!"

"Wrong, pretty lady. We're the first to own a television set!" Mother fell into the nearest chair.

> *"Wrong, pretty lady. We're the first to own a television set!" Mother fell into the nearest chair.*

Nevertheless, Mother discovered that she liked being the first lady in her neighborhood to own a television. It made her the queen of the airways and very popular. Men, women and children came to visit.

I even became popular when the "stuck-ups" at school lowered themselves to become my friends. I knew that it was only to have a chance to view the test pattern on the television, or maybe, if they were lucky, to see an actual show, but I enjoyed the attention anyway. Every member of the family did. Even Grandma arranged for a carload of her lady friends from the retirement center to come for a viewing.

My brother John wanted to charge admission. Mother vetoed that idea because she didn't think it was neighborly. We should have, though, because the carpets were ruined by muddy feet, the toilet was flushed a hundred times a day, our refrigerator was raided, towels got dirty, and the additional electrical usage nearly sent my parents into bankruptcy. There were even a few who thought we should feed them a nice meal since we were so rich and could afford a television set.

That first set looked exactly like a radio. It sat on the table and was enclosed in a wooden case shaped like the radio in the kitchen. The

difference was the gray-looking glass screen that dominated the front. When we turned it on, we were greeted by a loud humming sound and a screen that was filled with either black-and-white flashing dots or a round bull's-eye design called the "test pattern."

We set up as many chairs as possible in the room, and they were full an hour before the first show was to be broadcast. Family members had to fight for a seat. Mom even made me miss an episode of *The Lone Ranger* because the neighbor brought his in-laws to see our new wonder.

The lack of seating didn't stop people. Crowds stood at the window, hoping to catch a glimpse of movie stars without having to pay to see a movie.

It was like living in a fishbowl. After about a month of this, the glamour of being everyone's friend lost its shine.

We got our peace—and our house—back when the Gordons got a set. Theirs was better. The picture appeared larger because it was the type that reflected onto a mirror. I saw it once, but I liked ours better. The viewer had to slouch to see the type the Gordons had. But the neighbors liked theirs better. Besides, the living room at the Gordons' was much larger—and they kept a better supply of food.

Mom vacuumed the crumbs from under the cushions. Dad scrubbed the Kool-Aid stains out of the carpet—or at least as much as would come out. Sis and I counted the silverware; only three spoons and two forks were missing. John washed the nose- and fingerprints off the windows. Life finally returned to normal. ❖

Clayton Moore as the Lone Ranger with Jay Silverheels as Tonto are ready to thunder into action and set wrongs right. Photo by CBS Photo Archive, Getty Images

Shopping With Charlotte

By Larry Nestor

It was the summer of 1957. My family and I were visiting relatives in St. Louis, Mo., staying with my Uncle Mack and Aunt Sadie on the city's north end. My dad and brother, Don, left early one morning to go downtown. I would have gone along, but I liked to sleep in, especially during summer vacation.

After about an hour and a half, the phone rang. It was my dad, and he told me he had been on the *Shopping With Charlotte* TV show. He said he would tell us all about it when he got home.

In less than an hour, my dad and brother pulled up on DeSoto Street and parked. I waited as they came up the long flight of stairs to my aunt and uncle's apartment. My mom, Aunt Sadie and Uncle Mack joined us in the air-conditioned parlor. (My aunt and uncle only cooled their parlor/sitting room—but this kept down their electricity bills.) After catching his breath, my dad began to tell us the events of the morning as my brother chimed in now and then.

It seems they were walking down the street when they were approached by the show's producer. The show featured boxers and wrestlers, three of each, and it was short one wrestler. The woman told Dad that he would portray the needed wrestler.

Always loving a good joke, Dad didn't need much persuasion to go along with the gag. My brother was escorted to the control room because the studio was so small. Dad wanted to call and alert us about the show, but there was little time and no phone. Remember, this was long before cell phones.

The "contestants," each bigger than the last, lined up, my dad included. Charlotte opened the show by explaining to the viewers that three

She asked if my dad was a boxer or a wrestler. He responded, "I once wrestled a hamburger."

boxers and three wrestlers were being featured on the show. Then she went down the line and spoke to each man.

When she reached my dad, she asked his name, and if he was a boxer or a wrestler. He responded, "I once wrestled a hamburger." This caused Charlotte much chagrin, but my brother held his stomach and rolled with laughter in the control room.

Wooden chairs were put out, and Charlotte explained that they would play a game of musical chairs. The winner would receive a deluxe box of King's Men toiletries. The music started, and the men began to quickly circle the chairs.

One by one, contestants were eliminated, finally leaving my dad and a wrestler who easily weighed 350 pounds. The next time the music stopped, the two made a mad dash for the lone remaining chair. My dad claimed that he had more than 50 percent occupation of the chair, as the big guy caught only a small part of it with his ample backside. The chair broke apart, sending my dad and the huge wrestler onto the floor. By rights, my dad felt that he should have been awarded first prize.

But Charlotte was biased against Dad because of his earlier snappy comment. She said the big guy had won, but announced that she was going to award each a deluxe box of King's Men toiletries.

Later, when my dad opened the box, he saw that it was not the deluxe size. He called the show, but the producer said that was all they had. So my dad took it one step further. He contacted the manufacturer and told them what had happened. Now Dad had enough cologne to float a small boat.

I think I can still smell it on the hallowed walls where I now live. ❖

The First TV Remote

By Linda Loegel

Television came into my world in the middle of the night in 1950, when I was 10 years old. I was sleeping soundly when I felt someone shaking me in an effort to wake me. Barely opening one eye, I looked up in the darkness to see my mother and father bending over me, beaming with joy. They were thrilled about the new invention called "television" that they'd just witnessed at a neighbor's house, and they couldn't contain their excitement until morning. Cutting them off in midsentence, I mumbled, "That's nice," and rolled over and fell back to sleep.

By morning, however, I was quite awake, and my curiosity was aroused. I couldn't wait to see television for myself, so after dinner, Mom and Dad gladly took my sister, Donna, and me over to the neighbor's house. The four of us sat mesmerized by the action on the tiny black-and-white screen.

The author stands in front of her childhood home.

What a glorious sight it was to watch the *Gillette Friday Night Fights*! Before now, we had listened to them on the radio. But now we could actually see the boxers and referees, and we could almost feel each punch as it was thrown. The picture wasn't very clear by today's standards, but even with the snow, we found television exhilarating.

The next night found us once again at our neighbor's house, this time to watch wrestling.

Television soon became an addiction. Instead of spending our evenings at home listening to *Little Luigi* or *Amos 'n' Andy* on the radio, we were usually at someone else's house, watching programs like *Your Show of Shows* and *The Life of Riley*.

Just when I was beginning to think that we would be the only family in Springfield, Vt., that didn't own the modern miracle, our turn finally came. Mom and Dad proudly carried home a black-and-white Capehart television set. After carefully removing it from the cardboard box, they placed it in the corner of the living room next to the soon-to-be-abandoned console radio.

Dad headed outside and planted the long antenna pole firmly in the ground beside the back stoop. He then peered through the back window and patiently waited for instructions from Mom, Donna and me, who were stationed at various points between the stoop and the living room, ready to relay the word that the antenna was aimed in the right direction.

1952 Westinghouse ad, House of White Birches nostalgia archives

"How's that?" he asked Mom, who was standing in the laundry room on the other side of the window.

Mom asked Donna, who was standing in the kitchen, "Do you see anything yet?"

Donna then relayed the question to me. I was standing in the living room, my eyes glued to the fuzzy television screen.

"Almost, but not quite!" I yelled to Donna, who told Mom, who told Dad to give the antenna another slight turn.

"Hold it right there!" I shouted down the line as I heard the familiar *dum-de-dum-dum* and watched, entranced, as Jack Webb materialized on the snowy screen. The message reached Dad, and soon we were all crowded around the new television set to watch Det. Sgt. Joe Friday solve a crime.

Soon we were having breakfast in Hawaii with Arthur Godfrey and eating dinner in the Peanut Gallery with Howdy Doody and Buffalo Bob Smith.

Radio was never like this!

We performed our bucket-brigade routine, with Dad standing outside, ready to turn the antenna, every time we changed to one of the three channels that were available to us back then—except on rainy days. In bad weather, we watched whatever channel was already on so that Dad wouldn't have to get wet.

I guess you could say that we had the world's first remote channel changer. ❖

Our Favorite Shows

Chapter Four

The first time I ever saw the painting by Ben Kimberly Prins from *The Saturday Evening Post* (from the Oct. 4, 1958 issue) I had to smile. It brought back such memories! The department-store floors are empty with the exception of the third floor television department. Patrons are gathered there jammed around the display sets. The parking area is jam-packed. Even the yard man has left his mower to catch the World Series on TV.

I remember so well when my favorite show, first on radio and later on television, was always the playing of the World Series. "The boys of October" always could be counted on to bring us some thrills. Babe Ruth, Lou Gehrig, Ted Williams, Ty Cobb, Stan Musial, Mickey Mantle and dozens of other baseball heroes dotted the decades from the 1930s to the 1960s.

The first World Series game I can remember hearing was broadcast over a crackly radio signal. Years later I marveled when the Fall Classic was broadcast on TV, and we could see, as well as hear, the spectacular play-by-play.

Over the years, the readers of *Good Old Days* magazine have shared with us the stories of their favorite shows. From daytime soap operas to Western adventures, from drama to comedy, these programs were as varied as our readers. They would no more miss their favorite shows as the ardent baseball enthusiasts in the Prins painting. (I remember very well my grandmother refusing to move from her living room rocking chair until her favorite soap opera was finished.)

When we envisioned this book, we knew that we just had to share these wonderful nostalgic looks back at those favorites from radio and television. So return with us to the days when the World Series was the most-watched program to be found on the airwaves on a warm October afternoon. And while we're there, we'll take a look at the program guide and see some more of our favorite shows.

—*Ken Tate*

The Radio Rangers, Johnny Carson and Me

By Patty Flye Peavey with Ray Bush

E verybody remembers Johnny Carson as the "King of Late Night" and the longtime host of *The Tonight Show*. But I knew Johnny before he was famous, when he was a fledgling radio announcer, and I was a musician in Nebraska. Here's how it happened. I started performing when I was only 6 years old as a member of the musical Flye Family. We were heard on programs from KWTO Springfield, Mo., and KOAM Pittsburg, Kan.

At the age of 13, I began working with my sister Betty on the *Renfro Valley Barn Dance* program, broadcast over WHAS in Louisville, Ky. We were known professionally as "Betty and Pat."

Meanwhile, a talented quartet of musicians were regrouping after having served in World War II. In January 1946, Ray Bush, Kelland Clark, Eddie Sosby and Hal Clark returned from the Armed Forces,

Pictured left to right are Ray Bush, Dorwin "White" Whitlow, Patty Flye, Johnny Sapp and Eddie Sosby.

and along with Bob Norton, began playing clubs in Detroit and Chicago.

Later that year an offer came from KFAB in Lincoln, Neb., and The Radio Rangers band was formed. The leader was Eddie Moore Sosby; he kept the Sosby name from earlier days at WLW in Cincinnati, Ohio, where he had worked with Ray and Leonard Sosby in a trio known as The Sosby Brothers.

The original Radio Rangers featured Sosby on rhythm guitar; Bush on steel guitar; Kelland Clark, accordion; Hal Clark, lead guitar; and Norton, on bass. When Kelland Clark left for a different job, Tony Bigda joined the band as accordionist. Hal Clark—who wrote *I Dreamed of Hillbilly Heaven* and became well known in the Los Angeles area under the name of Hal Southern—and Bob Norton also decided to go elsewhere.

Harlan Cagle became the lead guitarist, and Dorwin "White" Whitlow became the bass player. White had worked at KWKH, Shreveport, La., and WRUP in Gainesville, Fla., with Toby Dowdy and The Jubilee Hillbillies; at Lafayette, La., with Doc Guidry and The Sons of Cajuns; and with an Air Force Special Services band.

Musicians seem to be a restless breed. Bigda decided to go back to Michigan, and eventually Cagle followed him. In May 1947, I arrived from *Renfro Valley Barn Dance* to join the group as accordionist and vocal soloist.

Also arriving that May was Johnny Sapp, who joined the Rangers after playing fiddle for Ted Daffin and Ernest Tubb. Johnny had worked with Daffin in Texas, and when Daffin left the band, Johnny led it for some time. Johnny was with Tubb on WSM for five years and played fiddle for Tubb's movies.

During this time, young Johnny Carson was attending the University of Nebraska and announcing our radio programs at KFAB. It was Johnny's first job after serving in the U.S. Navy.

He was a very good ventriloquist, I remember, and he went on various show dates with us, taking along Tommy, his wooden-headed pal.

On July 30, 1947, we did our radio show from a big farm near Waverly, Neb., scene of the state soil-terracing contest. Johnny Carson's first special program was presented there by KFAB before the plowing contest.

My favorite memory of Johnny is when he introduced me as "the lovely girlfriend of The Radio Rangers," describing in detail my bluish-gray dress, which had a full skirt with inserts of Indian design.

After my work with The Radio Rangers, I went back to *Renfro Valley* and then on to *The Ozark Jubilee* in Springfield, Mo. I continued with my music and was with *Renfro Valley Folks* from 1984 until it was sold in 1989.

And Johnny Carson? Well, you know what happened to him! ❖

Johnny Carson puts words into the mouth of Tommy. This photograph was taken by the author.

Remembering the Pinkster

By Lynne Larson

*W*hen I was a kid in the early 1960s, I adored Dorothy Provine, the perky blonde who lit up our Saturday nights as Pinky Pinkham, flapper extraordinaire, in a vintage TV series called *The Roaring 20's.* Not yet old enough or bold enough to actually paint the town ourselves, my adolescent friends and I would spend the evening watching Pinky strut her stuff at the imaginary Charleston Club, belting out such showstoppers as *Are You From Dixie?* and *Don't Bring Lulu* with all the sparkle and jolt of the bathtub gin she was presumably selling under the table.

This was the Jazz Age filtered through black-and-white TV, as inoffensive by today's standards as a church social, but Pinky couldn't have been better cast. Provine made us forget the fact that she was a theater arts major from Seattle rather than the reincarnation of the original "It Girl" from the inside of a 1920s vaudeville trunk. No one we knew of could dance like Pinky, who had the "ooo" of "boo-be-ba-doo" down to a science, complete with the requisite cloche hat, high cheekbones and those large, doleful eyes. She was the "Sweetheart of Sigma Chi"

> *The whole country was tuning in just to see the Pinkster bend her knees, twist her beads and say, "Boo-be-ba-doo!"*

and a sexy saloon hoofer rolled into one, and we girls, green with envy, hung on her every toe-tapping move.

Someone in a magazine once called her "the Pinkster," evoking the light, comedic quality Dorothy brought to the role. Whatever she was called, everyone within sight of a television screen on Saturday nights would stop and watch when the drums rolled her intro at the Charleston Club. My mother came in from the kitchen, and my dad looked up from the sports page. Even my older brother paused in his aloof stroll through the living room to catch Pinky's act. Something about it—and her—was irresistible.

If "Pinky Pinkham" sounds like just a bit of fluff and eye candy designed to frame an hour of cops and robbers, the character probably started out that way in the initial scripts. But something happened. Provine did Pinky so well that the sidekick showgirl became the main attraction, and soon the whole country was tuning in just to see the

Facing page: Actress and singer Dorothy Provine, the Pinkster, pictured in 1960.
Photo by Hulton Archive/Getty Images

Pinkster bend her knees, twist her beads, toe-tap through *Sweet Georgia Brown*, and say, "Boo-be-ba-*doo*, I'm the cat's pajamas, and so are you!" (If you're out there, Dottie, kudos to you. You were fabulous!)

Warner Brothers, the program's producer, suddenly recognized what it had and began to fatten her role. "Before long," read a 1961 article in *Time*, "if things go right, *The Roaring 20's* may consist of 50 minutes of Provine and five commercials, with screen credits superimposed on a shot of the St. Valentine's Day Massacre."[1]

Whether it was a wild rendition of *Black Bottom* or a poignant *Am I Blue?*, we were mesmerized. Dorothy had a vibrant voice, great rhythm, and of course, those cheekbones. But most of all, she had presence, that elusive gift that can't be taught, begged or borrowed—and she played it to the hilt with more than just shimmy and sex appeal. There was a sweetness too, an innocence that added vulnerability to her charm. Pinky had mastered the "come hither" look, slithering through a version of *Hard-Hearted Hannah* in a black sequined dress, but she made speakeasies seem almost wholesome.

In those days, we all wanted to be Pinky. There were Pinky paper dolls and Pinky lunch buckets. Cloche hats and string beads made a fashionable comeback. Songs from the 1920s became the rage. My girlfriends took dancing lessons until their soles wore through, and they learned how to "do the Raccoon" and shimmy from the knees down in true Pinky style. Alas, with few Charleston Clubs around, most of us ended up on the cheer squad, bouncing pom-poms for the football team, but it was fun while it lasted, as was the show itself.

A few months ago, my husband found an Internet link to some episodes of classic television. He was looking for *Rawhide* when over his shoulder I spotted *The Roaring 20's* a few titles down the list. I couldn't believe it! I hadn't thought of the show in 40 years. But with a few clicks of the mouse, there was Pinky at the Charleston Club again, belting out *California, Here I Come* with all the gusto I remembered.

I suddenly felt a bittersweet twinge for lost youth and simple pleasures and an innocence I can't retrieve. Old shows will do that. We associate them with events in our lives that coincide, like that first kiss, or your mom coming in from the kitchen and your dad looking up from the sports page, just to watch Pinky Pinkham sing *My Buddy* as if she meant every sentimental word. Funny … *The Roaring 20's* itself was a show that played on memories—the flapper, the fur coat, the nickel phone call—and now I was feeling nostalgic about the nostalgia, child of the 1960s that I was.

What finally caught my interest, though, was something else. After all this time, 45 years and counting, Pinky's musical numbers held up like a starched collar. The show built around her was grainy and dated by today's standards. The sets were tacky, the action limited, the production threadbare—except when Dorothy dashed on stage. Then, nothing else mattered. Pinky filled the screen as she had all those decades before, bouncing through a rousing *Mademoiselle From Armentières* and then crooning *Till We Meet Again* with those same soulful eyes.

Sentimental? Old-fashioned? Sure. But everyone in our living room was riveted to the computer screen until the songs ended.

I looked into my friends' faces, most of them as old as mine, and caught a glimpse of those long-ago Saturday nights. "Oh, I remember her!" said one woman. "I loved her!"

"So did I!" winked the husband at her side.

"Play it again, Sam," another friend joked. "I used to be crazy about that show. I learned to dance because of Dorothy. We *all* did. I'd forgotten how much fun it used to be. It's funny. Pinky's still cool, even in black-and-white."

Pinky *was* cool, *especially* in black-and-white. Some colors simply belong to their era. That night on YouTube, I learned something about comedic presence, classic characters, showstoppers and scene stealers. And I learned about nostalgia.

I was going to mention it to my friends, but just then Miss Provine launched heart and soul into *Baby Face*, and they couldn't take their eyes off the screen. Grainy video, dated set pieces, old-fashioned tunes, a lifetime of seeing television favorites come and go … at that moment, none of it mattered. The Pinkster was on stage again. ❖

The Gum That Won the West

By Michael Grogan

When P.K. Wrigley saw a singing cowboy draw 250,000 cheering fans in Ireland, he told his dad about it, and the chewing gum people signed that cowboy to star in a new 15-minute radio show called *Melody Ranch*. That singing, guitar-strumming cowhand was Gene Autry, and in the first two months of 1940, chewing gum sales rose significantly.

Gene's sponsor, Doublemint Gum, made a mint-flavored pack of chicle wrapped in a green band. It tasted like a cool country breeze, and Autry's commercials had a down-home flavor. In his low-pitched Texas-Oklahoma accent, he talked about how his sponsor's gum gave you a little lift—how it calmed jittery nerves. But the clincher was that you could enjoy a minty chew while leaving both hands free for whatever chores needed tackling.

Kids went around thinking Wyatt Earp had a chaw before each confrontation with armed desperadoes. It was gospel that Doublemint was part of a cavalry troop's daily supplies. When one of us got into a playground fracas, we hauled out a slab of gum and let our eyes bore into the bad kid's face. Our mouths shut meant we had been riled to the breaking point. (I had a tactic Gene Autry might not have approved of: I put my sticky wad of gum in my opponent's hair, which sort of immobilized him while I retreated.)

So I saved my money and bought a 20-pack box of this old Western standby. When I met

Gene Autry, was back in the saddle again with the Doublemint *Melody Ranch*, 1940–1942.

strangers in the neighborhood, I passed out the Doublemint and then sized up the newcomers while they field-stripped the chicle. Without a doubt, Wyatt Earp did the same thing.

In the hands of a shrewd operator, a stick of Doublemint became the ultimate weapon. You could drive stuffy adults crazy, stretching your gum with your hands. Dropping a lump on the carpet could start a range war.

Each Saturday night, circa 1947, when *Melody Ranch* lasted a half hour, we hurried to our radio to hear Gene sing *I'm Back in the Saddle Again*. I passed out the gum, and we listened to "genuine Western ballads" written by certified public accountants or barbers in western Detroit. Comic Pat Buttram, Gene's radio sidekick, sounded like a lump of petrified gum had lodged in his swaller-pipe.

We kids helped South American chicle growers become financially solvent. I am told that on some plantations, photos of Gene were hung on the walls. From the Wrigley plant in Chicago, a billion sticks of this all-American economic, social, philosophical and recreational panacea came scuttling down the conveyor belts.

When we got together on Monday after school to talk about Gene's movie, *Sons of New Mexico*, we studied the latest comic books—and someone inevitably broke out two packs of Doublemint. We chewed it, feeling the stream of succulent sugar explode all over our tongues. And somehow, we felt tall, brave and successful. ❖

Turn the Radio On

By Martha Baxley

*D*on't feel sorry for those of us who grew up without television. We had radio! Living near Red River, Texas, we got KRLD and WBAP out of Dallas, and WFAA out of Fort Worth. Infrequently, we picked up station XERA out of Del Rio, Texas, a strong station of 100,000 watts where the Carter family began in 1938. Our daily routine included news at 6 a.m., noon and 6 p.m., for the weather and market reports. The noon news was followed by one minute of rollicking Western music. A group of young men working at a flour mill used their lunch hour to race across town and play for free, signing off with "We're the Light Crust Doughboys from Burrus Mill!" After they got offers for concerts all over Texas, they became Bob Wills' Band.

Some newscasters were famous. Any celebrity worth his salt was mentioned by Walter Winchell, whose Sunday-night news opened with "Good evening, Mr. and Mrs. America and all the ships at sea!"

On a daily basis, we gathered at the radio to hear news of the war.

Most folks worked during the day, but housewives could listen to afternoon serials. The first, *Ma Perkins*, was sponsored by a soap company, so they were dubbed "soap operas." *Ma Perkins* was soon followed by *Easy Aces, Lorenzo Jones, Stella Dallas* and *Portia Faces Life*. Commercials were 30 seconds long, at the beginning and end of the show.

Kid shows started at 4 p.m. I never got home in time for *The Lone Ranger*, but I lapped up *Jack Armstrong—The All-American Boy*, sponsored by Wheaties, and *Little Orphan Annie*, sponsored by Ovaltine. I longed to breakfast on Wheaties, topped off with a glass of Ovaltine, but during the Great Depression, asking for store-bought items was a waste of breath.

My mother labeled them expensive and poor in quality, but she finally surrendered a quarter for a can of Ovaltine plus another quarter for an Orphan Annie decoder pin. The Friday program included a coded message of future events, which could be revealed only to those with a decoder pin. After I went through all the hassle to get one, I threw it away. It was hard to work, and it rusted, making it useless. Even worse, knowing what would happen ruined the story.

After we all pitched in with supper, we gathered in the living room. My stepfather sat beside the set to ceremoniously turn it on and change stations. My mother rested in her easy chair while I sat cross-legged on the floor in front of the set. In total silence we listened to variety shows: *Jack Benny* (Jell-O), *Fred Allen* ("Buy

Firestone Tires") and *Bob Hope* ("For a brighter smile, try Pepsodent").

My favorites were comedy monologues by Fanny Bryce as Baby Snooks, and Edgar Bergen, the only ventriloquist to succeed on radio, with his puppets Charlie McCarthy and Mortimer Snerd. When Kate Smith belted out *God Bless America*, she evoked patriotism I haven't seen since. Bob Burns became famous telling funny stories about his native state on *The Arkansas Traveler*. Burns was a trombone player. On his show he introduced his homemade horn, which he called a "bazooka," saying that it sounded something like a "wounded moose."

I liked situation comedies too. *Fibber McGee and Molly* relied on running gags with friends and neighbors like The Old-Timer, Mayor LaTrivia and local weatherman Foggy Williams. Fibber's hall closet was featured in every show. He never cleaned it out, and he always forgot and opened the door to a roaring avalanche—to the delight and glee of the studio audience.

And each week, in *The Aldrich Family*, teenage Henry Aldrich chased another pretty girl who spurned him, while his ever-wise, all-time friend Kathleen waited to pick up the pieces.

The Great Gildersleeve was a braggart and blusterer, but for a confirmed bachelor, he did a good job raising his orphaned niece and nephew. Each week was a lesson on coping with life while enjoying every minute of it.

Amos 'n' Andy featured lots of running gags. *Lum and Abner*, a forerunner of *Green Acres,* ran a country store with their oddball neighbors for customers. George Burns and Gracie Allen (no relation to Fred) were out-of-work vaudeville players who wandered into radio to become household names. Gracie was smart, but she played dumb on the show to an audience howling with laughter. When she died suddenly of a heart attack, George retired for a short time, but eventually returned to work in television and in movies. At age 81, he made the movie *Oh, God*. We all liked the *Jack Benny Show* with his

Phil Spitalny organized his first all-girl, 22 member, orchestra in 1933. Spitalny and the orchestra were the stars of the long-running The Hour of Charm *(1935–1948). Spitalny married Evelyn Kaye, known professionally as "Evelyn and Her Magic Violin." Peggy Ryan is also seen in this still from the 1945 Universal film* Here Come the Co-Eds.

real-life wife, Mary Livingstone, playing a character on the show, and singer Dennis Day and valet, Rochester, played by Eddie Anderson. The running gag about Jack's stinginess, including driving an old Maxwell, was strictly a joke, for in real life, he was generous and donated a whopping sum to his hometown, Waukegan, Ill.

Another weekly favorite, Bob Hope's *The Pepsodent Show*, with singer Frances Langford, had been on the air several years when World War II began. He quickly arranged to air his show live from as many of our Armed Forces bases as possible.

One Man's Family, a weekly drama about a wealthy family in San Francisco, had foghorns in the background. The large, three-generation family was well-educated, and they had perfect grammar, good jobs, nice cars and lovely homes. They truly loved one another, never quarreled and spent all their spare time getting together. Being from a broken home myself, I looked forward to each episode.

The Shadow by Mario DeMarco,
courtesy House of White Birtches nostalgia archives

Ah, quiz shows! On *The $64 Question*, starting with a $2 question, contestants doubled their money with each correct answer up to $64. On *Dr. I.Q.*, a correct response won a carton of Mars Bars. On Ralph Edward's *Truth or Consequences*, failing to answer his question rated a stunt, like fighting your way out of a paper bag or singing while drinking a glass of water.

Saturday night offered *Grand Ole Opry*, which first took to the airwaves in the mid-1920s. We also listened to swing bands: Horace Heidt and His Musical Knights, Kay Kyser, Glenn Miller, Tommy Dorsey, Skinnay Ennis, and Guy Lombardo and The Royal Canadians.

Saturday Night Hit Parade featured popular songs of the week sung by big-name stars. Sunday night, after listening to the re-enactment of a current movie, we heard—all the way from Chicago—Phil Spitalny and His All-Girl Orchestra, featuring Evelyn and her "magic violin" solo.

Saturday afternoons featured sports events. During the World Series, baseball fans carried small radios to work. For special boxing matches, people who didn't have a radio went to the neighbors to listen. Drop-ins were welcome, and everybody gathered around the set to munch popcorn and listen—but no talking!

In 1937, new kid Joe Louis challenged world-boxing champion Max Schmeling. Two minutes into the first round, with his first hard punch, Joe Louis knocked Schmeling out, and the world went wild!

After a few feverish announcements, the regularly scheduled program came on—and we heard a knock at our door. We opened it to find a young couple who had walked two miles to hear that fight, and now they fought back tears of disappointment. My parents asked them to stay for the regular program. My mother served cake and coffee, and later, my stepfather drove them home.

Popular mystery shows such as *Mr. District Attorney*, *I Love a Mystery* and *Calling All Cars* taught us that "Crime does not pay." *The Inner Sanctum Mysteries* was introduced by a rusty door clanging shut, while *The Shadow* opened with an eerie whistle as a hollow voice whispered, "The Shadow knows!"

Once when we had overnight guests, one young visitor suggested we listen to *Lights Out*. We had never heard of it, and with good reason. It aired at 11:30 on Saturday nights, and we never stayed up that late—but after hearing her vivid description, we all wanted to hear.

The grown-ups retired, leaving a covey of young girls to settle in and listen. At the first notes of the spooky theme music, our guest snapped off the light, vowing that the story was better in the dark.

A half-dozen girls sat cross-legged on the floor, a semicircle of young statues in the faint light of the radio dial. The show was eerie enough to give us a good scare, and we went to bed to sleep soundly.

After that, *Lights Out* became a weekly feature for my sister and me. Then, one Saturday, she had a date, but I wanted to listen to it. At bedtime, my mother gave me a long, measuring look. Facing a freckle-faced 12-year-old in flannel pajamas and fuzzy slippers, she went to bed, shaking her head.

To further prove my maturity, I pulled the little cord to turn off the single bulb on the ceiling. Feeling grown-up in the glow from the radio, I sat in Mother's easy chair and crossed my ankles as eerie music introduced the goriest story imaginable! Saws severed bones to the accompaniment of moans, groans, whimpers, sobs and blood-curdling screams.

Wide-eyed, with my hand on the knob, I sat frozen to the end—but at the first note of the theme music, I snapped off the radio. Too late I realized I had trapped myself in total darkness. With no hope of finding the string dangling from the single ceiling light, I stoically groped my way through the darkness into the hall. Already spooked, I trapped myself between doors, bumping into them in a series of booming crashes.

I finally scampered to my bed and dove headfirst under the covers. Trying to block out the screams and moans that were replaying in my head, it took ages for me to go to sleep—and I never again listened to *Lights Out*.

In 1938, one mystery show made history. Directed by and starring Orson Welles, *War of the Worlds* featured invading Martians armed with ray guns and ultramodern spaceships. As part of the play, at crucial points, a radio announcer broke in with simulated "news bulletins" that seemed to indicate that earth was being invaded by weird aliens! Evacuate New York! Take to the hills!

On that day, the highway to the beach was filled. One couple tuned in just in time to hear Welles' warnings to evacuate. Convinced that it was for real, they raced along the freeway, warning others of a Martian invasion.

People fled New York City in a panic, causing the worst traffic jam in history. The new Holland Tunnel became one solid traffic jam of hysterical people screaming, fainting and sobbing in fear.

In 1940, we listened on the radio as the

200,000
FOR BREAKFAST
with Tom Breneman

Above: Tom Breneman hosted Breakfast at Sardi's, *a live informal show, from Sardi's restaurant at Hollywood and Vine in Hollywood, Calif. Below: Dolores Reade Hope laughs with Tom after commenting, "You'd expect a man who's had breakfast with 200,000 women to be in the general condition of butter at a wartime rummage sale ... but Tom bears up amazingly well." Photos courtesy* Breakfast at Sardis.

Democratic National Convention nominated Franklin Roosevelt for an unheard-of third term as president. On Election Day, we listened again to the reports that he had won by a landslide.

I was listening to a symphony at 2 p.m. on Dec. 7, 1941, when an announcer broke in to announce the bombing of Pearl Harbor. The next day, our school body gathered to listen as Congress declared war on Japan.

Thereafter, on a daily basis, we gathered at the radio to hear news of the war. We listened in stunned disbelief to reports of Japanese wartime atrocities, including the Bataan Death March, and the fall of the Philippines.

We agonized through the Battle of the Coral Sea and the German invasion of Africa and Italy. During a very bad winter, the war news focused on the Battle of the Bulge in Europe. We knew neighbor boys who were there. One of them came home in a wheelchair after his frozen feet were amputated. Another came home suffering from shell shock from which he never recovered.

Our troops' bloody invasion of Normandy on D-Day, June 6, 1944, had begun to bring an end to the war in Europe. My husband, Glenn, was stationed at an Army base in New Orleans, and I was there with him. Houses were separated only by narrow driveways, and before the days of central air, we slept with open windows. He woke me at 3 a.m. that momentous day, excited because the Allies had invaded France at Normandy. Convinced he was dreaming, I countered, "How could you know?"

"The man next-door listened to his radio all night!" he exclaimed.

A few weeks later, we heard Roosevelt agree to a fourth term as president. Then, on the radio, we learned of his death on April 12, 1945. I could not remember any other president. The next day, we heard Harry Truman being sworn into office. And in August 1945, the radio reported that the United States was using an atomic bomb on Hiroshima to end the war.

In the election year of 1948, the press was snobbish and cruel to Harry Truman, ridiculing his Missouri hat, folksy philosophy and oatmeal for breakfast. Following Roosevelt was no easy task, but he finished the term smoothly and ended the war. Nonetheless, people of status thought Thomas Dewey should win the presidency at the next election.

On that next Election Day, reporters announced returns in terms of "President-elect Dewey" receiving so many votes and "Truman," so many. But the common people spoke at the polls, and they rejoiced when Truman was declared winner by a landslide. My favorite memento at the Truman Library was a picture of him holding a preprinted newspaper that screamed "Dewey Defeats Truman" in a huge headline. Truman's grin seemed wider than his face.

Housewives worked with one ear to the radio. Hours flew as we did humdrum cooking, cleaning, sewing, and ironing. Aunt Susan offered new recipes, disc jockeys had music for every taste, and each morning, Arthur Godfrey growled, "Hello there! It's a pretty nice kind of a day!" with new talent and comments on current events.

Ken Murray's *Queen for a Day* was a must, for each day, one woman, chosen for being brave, kind, hardworking, or all the above, was rewarded with a salon makeover, a new wardrobe and a plane trip to Hollywood to appear on the show. One lady who appeared on his show was Mrs. Ada McKinney from Delight, Ark., my mother-in-law.

But all good things must come to an end. Hailing television as the second coming, we callously pushed the radio aside. But no matter how vividly TV portrays a story, something is lacking. Radio fostered a factor that television never bothers with. We listened. Because we learned to listen at an early age, we listened to our parents and our teachers. Because we listened, we were studious, well-behaved students who grew up to be hardworking, achieving adults—the generation that fought and won World War II.

As we listened to our favorite shows, we envisioned the characters. I truly loved *One Man's Family*, for as I listened, these people were vivid in my mind; but on TV, they looked like a bunch of kooks. Disappointed, I refused to watch it. I wasn't the only one who felt that way, for the program was soon dropped.

Television really was a giant step backward, for it leaves nothing to the imagination. ❖

Roy Acuff and the Grand Ole Opry

By Wayne Daniel

adio was a brand-new entertainment medium in 1925, when station WSM in Nashville made its first broadcast. In those days before network programming and the extensive broadcasting of recorded music, live entertainment was the staple fare of radio stations.

Anyone who could whistle, sing or play an instrument—from handsaw to grand piano—was almost assured an opportunity to appear before the microphone.

Among the many musicians willing to display their talents on the radio were the numerous fiddlers, banjo pickers, guitarists, yodelers and mountain singers whose specialty was a type of music called "hillbilly," later to be known as "country music."

Uncle Jimmy Thompson, an 80-year-old fiddler from the hills of Tennessee, decided that he would like to practice his craft on Nashville's newest radio station. He was allowed to go on the air at 8 p.m. on Saturday night, Nov. 28, 1925.

He had wanted to be a professional baseball player, but a sunstroke forced him to seek another career.

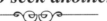

The response to Thompson's fiddling was immediate and immense. Listeners called in to the station, sent telegrams and wrote letters, all expressing their appreciation of the music. As a result of this outpouring of enthusiasm, Thompson was asked to return the following Saturday night to present another program of fiddle tunes, of which he had an inexhaustible supply.

The announcer at WSM the night Uncle Jimmy Thompson made his radio debut was George D. Hay. Known to his listeners as "the Solemn Old Judge," Hay had been born in Attica, Ind., in 1895.

He had worked as a newspaper reporter and as an announcer at WLS in Chicago before taking a job at WSM. He recognized the worth of the American folk music that was so much a part of the repertoire of country musicians like Uncle Jimmy Thompson. Hay was receptive to other hillbilly musicians seeking a chance to play on the radio, and soon the Saturday night fiddling was supplemented by performers on other stringed instruments, by harmonica players, square-dance callers and vocalists.

Facing page: June Carter performs with Roy Acuff during a Grand Ole Opry broadcast in 1956. (Photo by Yale Joel/Time & Life Pictures/Getty Images)

Hay first called his expanded Saturday night radio show the *WSM Barn Dance*, but soon gave it the name by which is it known today—the *Grand Ole Opry*, the oldest continuously broadcasting radio show on the air.

Hay adopted the practice of beginning each broadcast of the *Grand Ole Opry* with a toot on a steamboat whistle. He closed each show with a bit of homespun whimsy by telling listeners:

"That's all for now friends,
Because the tall pines pine
And the pawpaws pause,

And the bumblebees bumble all around.
And the eavesdropper drops
The grasshopper hops
While gently the ole cow slips away.
George D. Hay saying,
So long for now."

Most of the acts on the early *Grand Ole Opry* programs were string bands like The Gully Jumpers, The Possum Hunters, The Fruit Jar Drinkers and The Clod Hoppers. The few featured vocalists who came later included Uncle Dave Macon, who joined the Opry cast in 1926;

Ryman Auditorium, home of the Grand Ole Opry.
Photo by Donnie Beauchamp courtesy Nashville Convention & Visitors Bureau.

the Delmore Brothers, who came aboard in 1932; and Zeke Clements, who also became a member in the early 1930s.

But the man who started the *Grand Ole Opry* on its way to becoming a showcase for vocal talent was Roy Acuff. Born 1903 in Maynardville, Tenn., Acuff had wanted to be a professional baseball player, but a severe sunstroke in 1929 forced him to seek another career.

His parents and grandfather were musicians, and while recuperating from his illness, Acuff taught himself to play one of the instruments that was handy—the fiddle.

He was inspired by records of hillbilly artists Fiddlin' John Carson, Gid Tanner and The Carter Family. By listening to his sister, a semi-professional light opera singer, he learned how to achieve a powerful vocal delivery. As a result, his became one of the first strong voices in country music.

Encouraged by the success of his musical endeavors, Acuff dared to venture into the world of the professional musician. A stint with a medicine show was followed by performances in string bands.

By 1936, Roy Acuff and his band, the Crazy Tennesseans, had achieved enough regional popularity from performances on a Knoxville, Tenn., radio station to land a recording contract with the American Record Co.

They recorded *The Great Speckled Bird*, a song with spiritual lyrics and a traditional country tune; the Carter Family's *I'm Thinking Tonight of My Blue Eyes*; Hank Thompson's *Wild Side of Life*; and Kitty Wells' *It Wasn't God Who Made Honky-Tonk Angels*.

When Acuff tried out for a spot on the *Grand Ole Opry* in 1938, his soulful rendition of *The Great Speckled Bird* resulted in such tremendous mail response from listeners that he was asked to become a full-time member of the show.

In 1938, the *Grand Ole Opry* was heard for several hours each Saturday night on Nashville's WSM, a clear-channel, 50,000-watt station that could be picked up by radios in two-thirds of the country. The *Opry*, which originally had been broadcast from the WSM studio without a live audience, was also a stage show that attracted thousands of paying fans every Saturday night.

In October 1939, Acuff and his fellow Opry performers became even more widely known when the R.J. Reynolds Tobacco Co. decided to sponsor a 30-minute segment of the *Grand Ole Opry* on the National Broadcasting Co. radio network.

Acuff became a star performer on the show that advertised Prince Albert smoking tobacco. Other artists heard on the program, which remained on NBC for almost 20 years, included Minnie Pearl, Zeke Clements, the Duke of Paducah, Eddy Arnold, Ernest Tubb, Rod Brasfield, Red Foley and the Old Hickory Singers. Broadcasts of *The Prince Albert Show* began with the theme song:

Howdy, all you friends and neighbors,
Join us on the Prince Albert Show.
Tune up the five-string banjo,
Take down the fiddle and the bow.
Roll back the rugs on the floor,
Light up the old cob pipe.
Everyone will have some fun
At the Grand Ole Opry tonight.

In addition to being a radio star, Roy Acuff was also in demand as a stage performer. He took his shows to the largest concert houses in the United States and overseas. He was a major recording artist, and during the height of his career, he was seen in several Hollywood movies, including one called *Grand Ole Opry*.

In addition to *The Great Speckled Bird*, Acuff's most popular songs included *The Precious Jewel*, *Wabash Cannonball*, *Wreck on the Highway*, *Fireball Mail* and *Blue Eyes Crying in the Rain*.

After joining the Opry, Acuff began calling his band The Smoky Mountain Boys (there have also been some Smoky Mountain Girls). The band has had many members over the years, including Dobra player Pete "Bashful Brother Oswald" Kirby, banjoist Rachel Veach, fiddlers Tommy Magness and "Howdy" Forrester, and harmonica player Jimmy Riddle.

Roy Acuff, long known as "the King of Country Music," lived in a house on the grounds of Opryland, the Nashville theme park inspired by the Grand Ole Opry, up until his death Nov. 23, 1992. He was elected to the Country Music Hall of Fame in 1962, the first living performer to be so honored. ❖

Ding Dong School

By Jan Holden

I raised my kids with Mr. Rogers, and I admit that I enjoyed him right along with them. But I must confess that no teacher in the world could equal dear Miss Frances, and no classroom, real or imaginary, was as fascinating as *Ding Dong School*. Miss Frances was an apple-cheeked woman with twinkling eyes and a friendly smile. Though she couldn't have been very old, her conservative clothing and matronly figure gave her a grandmotherly charm. At least that's the way I remember her.

The NBC television cameras brought Miss Frances (whose real name was Frances Horwich) into my life in the mid-1950s, but the program debuted in Chicago on Oct. 3, 1952. Within six months, *Ding Dong School* was such an overwhelming success that Miss Frances could be seen from coast to coast. The program was first sponsored by Scott Paper Co. and later by General Mills Inc.

I could almost hear Miss Frances asking, "did you follow directions?"

Miss Frances brought excellent credentials to her TV classroom. She was, after all, a real teacher. The University of Chicago graduate obtained a master's degree from Columbia University, and in 1942, a doctorate in education from Northwestern University. She went on to become head of the education department at Chicago's Roosevelt College. And yet, despite her impressive academic background, Miss Frances knew just how to talk to little children.

When I was about 6 years old, Miss Frances taught me how to grow a sweet potato and turn it into a beautiful green plant. I remember feeling pretty special when Mom put my potato plant on the coffee table.

But I soon discovered that other kids watched Miss Frances too. My best friend, Barbara, also had watered a sweet potato, and the green shoots on her potato looked just as big and healthy as mine did. And so I learned another lesson from Miss Frances: Everyone has talents and abilities. And I—well, I was just one of Miss Frances' many admirers.

Fact is, Miss Frances received thousands of fan letters each week. I didn't know what a fan letter was back then, but I was delighted to receive a personal reply when I wrote to her in care of NBC.

The funny thing was, I didn't know until years later that Mom, who was also a teacher, had written her own fan letter to Miss Frances. As much as I adored Miss Frances, I supposed she didn't have anything to teach someone as wise as my own mother. But Mom told me good teachers were always looking for new ideas to bring "freshness" to the same things they taught year after year.

Mom appreciated the way Miss Frances stressed respect and responsibility. Kids who watched *Ding Dong School* were encouraged to help out by picking up their toys, caring for pets, and even helping with simple household chores.

I guess Miss Frances had a message for people of all ages.

Miss Frances also encouraged kids to be creative. Though my artistic abilities were minimal, I was always excited to try a new *Ding*

Miss Frances, my favorite teacher from the Good Old Days, finger-painting.

Dong School project. On one program, Miss Frances told us we'd be making something special out of pipe cleaners. She showed us how to make all sorts of cute animals by bending and twisting them.

At the end of the program, she encouraged us to run out to our local five-and-dime and purchase the inexpensive pipe cleaners. I was devastated when the clerk at our local store

told me he'd already sold them all to the other boys and girls who'd also been watching.

Another project involved finger paints. I remember her talking about the fun we could have just letting our fingers glide across a sheet of paper, and how even a child's tiny fist could create all sorts of interesting shapes and designs.

I guess one of Miss Frances' most basic lessons was that fun didn't demand a lot of money. We could have loads of fun floating a leaf like a tiny boat in a puddle. According to our *Ding Dong School* teacher, children didn't need lots of expensive toys, but materials that would stimulate young imaginations.

My fondest recollections are from the special times Mom and I spent trying Miss Frances' ideas. I remember Mom helping me make a stick horse out of an old broomstick and one of Dad's argyle socks.

I also remember how Mom would tiptoe into the room during the program's last few minutes and sit with me while Miss Frances told parents a few things about her program. Sometimes Miss Frances would tell parents to send us kids out to play so that she could speak just with the grown-ups. I don't know exactly what she shared with my mom, but I imagine it had something to do with encouraging us to use good manners, to learn to be more independent, and perhaps to help us grow up to be more secure boys and girls.

Sometimes when I wasn't sharing, or when I lost my temper, Mom would remind me that Miss Frances wouldn't approve. It didn't always work, but it certainly gave Mom an ally. I could almost hear Miss Frances asking, "Did you follow directions? Did you hang your coat up when you came indoors from play? Did you offer to help Mom set the dinner table? Good for you! Miss Frances is proud of her boys and girls!"

Those *Ding Dong School* days are long gone. But I don't think I'll ever forget my television teacher, who smiled and rang an old-fashioned handbell. That sound was always a happy one, and it promised good times with Miss Frances. ❖

The All-American Boy

By Charles Holt

Among the most memorable things from the Good Old Days were the radio adventure programs that played in the 1930s and 1940s. Everyone had his or her favorite: *Captain Midnight*, *Terry and the Pirates*, *Tom Mix*, *Hop Harrigan*, *Little Orphan Annie*, *Buck Rogers* and *The Lone Ranger*, to name just a few.

My favorite, and that of untold thousands of other kids, was the all-American boy from Hudson High. Can there be a kid of that generation who does not remember: "Jack Armstrong! Jack Armstrong! Jack Armstrong! The All-American Boy! Wheaties, Breakfast of Champions, brings you the thrilling adventures of Jack Armstrong, The A-l-l-l-l-American Boy!"

Or what about the Hudson High fight song? "Wave the flag for Hudson High, boys. Show them how we stand! Ever shall our team be champions, known throughout the land!"

The *Jack Armstrong* show was one of the longest running of the 1930s and 1940s radio thrillers. It began in 1933 and ran for almost 20 years. Beginning as a daily 15-minute serial, it later expanded to a full half-hour show. A generation of kids rushed home from school and raced through their after-school chores to be sitting in front of the family radio for the beginning of Jack's next exciting adventure.

What would it be? Would he and pals Bill and Betty foil another evil plot by some dastardly German spy to disrupt the nation's war effort? Would they set out upon another perilous trek through the jungles of deepest Africa to unravel some dark mystery?

Jack Armstrong publicity photo, House of White Birches nostalgia archives

Would Jack, using one of his many remarkable skills, fly them on a mission of mercy to rescue victims of flood, fire or other disasters? Would they help the FBI or G-men catch some gang of villainous counterfeiters or black marketeers?

Or would he be back at Hudson High, quarterbacking his team to another edge-of-the-seat, last-minute victory? The only certain thing was that, in the end, right would prevail, and the good guys would win.

In addition to the daily adventure stories, these programs offered their youthful listeners a plethora of nearly irresistible premiums, as they were called. *Jack Armstrong* was one of the more prolific. For one or two Wheaties box tops and 10 cents, you could send to General Mills for all sorts of things: secret-compartment rings, glow-in-the-dark dragon's-eye rings, encoding/decoding wheels for sending and receiving secret messages, aircraft identification cards, pedometers to encourage healthy walking, and "Breakfast of Champions" cereal bowls, to name just a few.

Sadly, very little of all this survives. Most has been lost or broken, or has just gone to that mysterious place where most of our kid stuff went. But what a delight it is when, browsing through some antiques-and-collectibles store, one comes across one of them. Unfortunately, rather than box tops and dimes, the cost is more likely to be $20 or $30 or more.

Of all the premiums Jack offered his radio buddies, my all-time favorites were the Tru-Flite flying models of World War II fighter planes, which Wheaties and *Jack Armstrong* offered in 1944. For a Wheaties box top—or "reasonable facsimile"—and 10 cents, I received a set of two models, usually an American or British plane paired with a German or Japanese one.

These were printed on cardboard stock and had about a 10-inch wingspan. We cut them out with scissors or a razor blade, and glued the pieces together according to remarkably detailed instructions. Then we glued a penny in the nose for balance. The planes could be thrown by hand to maneuver and sail across the yard, or

flown round and round by a string tied to the leading edge of the wing.

Altogether, 14 models were offered, including the P-40 Flying Tiger, Japanese Zero, P-47 Thunderbolt, British Spitfire, Russian Stormovik, German Focke-Wulf and Bell P-39 Airacobra.

I have no idea how many boxes of Wheaties I wolfed down to get box tops, or how many dimes I begged to send off to *Jack Armstrong* and General Mills for these wonderful models. Nor do I recall the number of hours of fun spent building and flying them. I can't guess how many were destroyed in furious air battles fought in the hotly contested skies over our backyard. They hold a very special place in my boyhood memories, but like most of the other treasures from that time, they are gone forever.

The **Jack Armstrong** *show was one of the longest running of the 1930s and 1940s radio thrillers.*

Or so I thought until I visited the Smithsonian Air and Space Museum in Washington, D.C., a few years ago. To my amazement, there, in the museum gift shop, were displayed for sale these very same Jack Armstrong Tru-Flite models. I could hardly believe my eyes!

I learned that they were being reprinted and sold to help support air museums such as the Smithsonian. The sales clerk said that they had trouble keeping them in stock, which was easy for me to understand since I bought a number of complete sets myself. I have given a few models to discerning friends and have lovingly built a few and flown several carefully controlled memorial flights in the backyard. The rest occupy an honored place among my various other kid treasures and memorabilia.

A historical note included in the individual kits sold at the museum provides some interesting background on these models. They were designed for General Mills by an Englishman named Rigby, and they began to be produced in 1944. In addition to offering them to listeners of the *Jack Armstrong* radio program, General Mills gave thousands to wounded servicemen during World War II to build and fly while recuperating. General Mills even organized national contests and gave awards for the best appearance, maneuverability and longest flights. ❖

Ma Perkins, Radio Adventuress

By Ed Knapp

In 1934, at the rascally age of 10, I was forever seeking high adventure and excitement. The home entertainment center, the radio, helped me fulfill that compulsive need. Every weekday after grade-school classes were excused, I would dart home with the speed and intensity of a wild stallion. Never but once did I fail to arrive in time to turn on the trusty five-tube radio in the living room to listen to a series of children's 15-minute adventure programs, including *Buck Rogers*, *Jack Armstrong—The All-American Boy*, *Tom Mix*, *Dick Tracy*, radio's *Little Orphan Annie*, *Don Winslow* and many more.

When I arrived home, breathless, I found the walnut-colored wooden radio cabinet still warm. Perhaps only minutes before, my mother had turned off the set after listening to a series of 15-minute adult dramas. They were commonly known as "soap operas," and rightly so, as they were sponsored in large part by soap companies. These "soaps," which Mom enjoyed with a passion, were heavily embroidered with family clashes, lost loves, tragic events, tearful partings and angry exchanges, all leaving deep emotional wounds. These trials and tribulations went on five days a week, month in and month out, with few solutions.

> *The announcer reminded us to "Tune in tomorrow"—as if he had to tell us!*

I learned about their sad content one day when I was sick and unable to go to school. Those sad soaps didn't impress me. I couldn't understand what she found so fascinating about those endless tales filled with heartache. I couldn't avoid hearing about the unhappy relationships and other woes, even far off in my bedroom upstairs. Mother had the radio volume turned up extra loud so she could do all her household cleaning—upstairs, downstairs and even in the basement—without missing a single melodramatic word.

Certainly I knew there was a world of difference between what Mom liked to listen to and what I enjoyed. I was so glad I got home in the latter part of the afternoon, when I could be transported to my world of adventure heroes. Their tales of surprise, intrigue and suspense kindled my young imagination, sparking imagery as real as life itself. It made such an impression on us when we were young that today, as senior citizens, we still remember those long-ago radio adventures.

Summer, when school was closed for three months, was wonderful. The longer days went well with all the things we had to do: skinny-dipping in the old mill pond, bicycle riding, sand-lot baseball, Saturday-afternoon movie matinees, picnics, games like Kick the Can and Hide-and-Seek, and sandpit BB-gun skirmishes ("Don't shoot your eye out!"). The only thing I didn't like about it was the fact that most of my 15-minute radio adventure programs left the airwaves until fall. I missed them as much as I would have missed a close playmate who had left town for the summer. I couldn't wait for their return.

I remained a dedicated radio serial-adventure enthusiast for several years. In 1938, when I was 14, summer again arrived, school closed, and as usual, my action radio friends left the air until late September.

That year, I had an invitation to visit my aunt in Chicago. I figured that without the company of my favorite radio friends, I might as well go visit my relatives and see the city. I soon made friends with some of the interesting neighborhood children. We had fun with jai alai paddle contests, marble games, sidewalk chalk, setting off firecrackers and going to the neighborhood movie house.

One afternoon, most of my new friends had gone hither and yon, leaving me to my own devices. There didn't seem much to do but loll about in Auntie's apartment. She had the same fascination with radio soap operas as did her sister, my mother. She had just tuned in Oxydol's *Ma Perkins*, a highly acclaimed series among the soaps. Aimlessly, I flopped onto her flowered-patterned couch while she worked on laundry. It seemed like it was going to be a very boring afternoon. I didn't figure it would be proper for me to turn the radio dial to another station, so I steeled myself for the domestic dribble I was sure would follow.

I made an effort to pay little attention to the *Ma Perkins* broadcast, but something in the story line caught my attention. Seems that a traveling circus had come to Rushville Center (Ma's hometown), and the gorilla cage door had been left open. The huge, menacing beast had escaped, and its whereabouts were unknown.

Rushville's inhabitants were alerted to the danger with emergency radio bulletins. That day's episode ended on that note. I was beginning to get interested.

Radio's perennial warm-hearted Ma Perkins (actress Virginia Payne) as she appeared in her airwaves character (1933–1960).

Hungry for adventure, I was in front of the radio set with my aunt the next day. When the program began, the narrator explained that the rampaging gorilla had wandered into Ma's neighborhood. Entering the open front door of Ma's two-story house, the gorilla had climbed the stairs to the second floor. Ma was in the backyard, tending her flower garden.

Ma soon strolled back into the house and started to go upstairs to get some needle-point she wanted to finish. Then, just as she started climbing the steps, the program ended. The announcer reminded us to "Tune in tomorrow"—as if he had to tell us!

My aunt and I could hardly wait to tune in at 3:15 p.m. the following day. It was almost as good as listening to my after-school adventure programs. The story picked up where it had left off. Ma was climbing the stairs, unaware of what awaited her. When she was halfway up the stairs, the telephone rang, so she turned and came back down to answer it. Then, once again, the episode ended as Ma headed upstairs.

My aunt and I were beside ourselves. *Ma Perkins* was a five-day-a-week soap. When would it ever end?

The following day, the story once more picked up with Ma heading upstairs. This time, her ascent was interrupted by a knock at the front door. Ma answered the door and was introduced to a salesman hawking his wares. Ma was busy but too kind to turn him away. She took the time to listen to him, then showed him out—and the program ended! It was Friday, and *Ma Perkins* wouldn't air again until Monday!

I never did learn the outcome, because I returned home on Saturday. But that occasion changed my young mind somewhat about soap operas. Sometimes they *weren't* dull.

I guess I'll never learn if Ma ever climbed those stairs and came face-to-face with the snarling gorilla, and what happened next. However, *Ma Perkins* remained on the air for the next 22 years (until 1960), so there must have been some solution to the peril she faced back then.

I never understood why the story moved along so slowly—until I realized that for the sponsor, it meant listeners, and the sale of more laundry soap. Ma Perkins had become an adventuress, and she had a new, young fan. ❖

Above: The author (right) with a friend dressed for Sunday school in 1934 in Chicago, Ill. Below: Virginia Payne poses in a publicity photo for the Ma Perkins *radio program.*

My Other Family, the Barbours

By Vernal Lind

*I*t all began one Sunday afternoon in January 1949 when I was 12 years old. "Why don't you kids go down and see Grandma this afternoon?" Mother suggested. "She'll be feeling lonesome." I lived with my family on a farm in the Leaf Hills of Minnesota. Grandma was now alone in the little house down the hill. Grandpa had died a few weeks before. That Sunday, Grandma would be alone for the first time.

Sunday was always a day of rest: church and Sunday school in the morning, with a big dinner at noon, followed by an afternoon of rest and quiet, unless company came or we went visiting. Sunday afternoons were uneventful, even boring, for my two younger sisters and me.

Grandma was delighted when she greeted us at the door. We had always made frequent visits to Grandma in her little house. As a treat, we could listen to the radio. That Sunday began a relationship. I turned the dial to WDAY Fargo, the NBC affiliate. We heard the announcer's introduction: "*One Man's Family*, dedicated to the mothers and fathers of the younger generation and to their bewildering offspring." Immediately, I became fascinated with this new radio family.

> *This family was like my own—so very real—yet their adventures were far more interesting.*

Though the program was then in its 18th year (it first aired April 29, 1932), I learned the family history by bits and pieces. This family was like my own—so very real—yet their adventures were far more interesting, even exciting. The cousins and aunts and uncles joined the ranks of my cousins and aunts and uncles.

In my mind I saw the Golden Gate Bridge and San Francisco Bay as the fog rolled in. I entered 264 Sea Cliff Drive, San Francisco, the large family home of the Barbours. I saw myself in the garden with Father Barbour. After all, he had a whole city lot devoted to his beautiful flowers. Father Barbour (J. Anthony Smythe) became the grandfather I no longer had. He grunted and complained and gave good advice—at least part of the time.

Mother Barbour (Minetta Ellen) became another kindly grandmother. The Barbours had five children, and both my parents had come from families of five children.

Paul Barbour (Michael Raffetto), with his deep voice, was a man I admired. He was the one most in tune with the younger generation and gave the best guidance and advice. At the same time, I dreamed of becoming a writer, and Paul was also a writer.

Living one block down and two blocks over were Hazel (Bernice Berwin) and Dan Murray and their children. Margaret was in the same grade—seventh—as I was. There were older twin brothers: Hank, who was the model student and did everything right; and Pinky, who always got into all kinds of trouble. Pinky added spice to the story.

Then there was Clifford, who seemed to be at odds with Father Barbour and the other family members. The excitement of those first months was Clifford's accident. As a result, he had partial amnesia, and 11 years of family problems were erased from his memory. But something good came out of this accident. Clifford paid more attention to his family and to the young son he had ignored for so many years.

Clifford's twin sister, Claudia, married to Nicholas Lacey, seemed to have had an exciting life. I learned that years before, she had eloped, and then her husband had died. Daughter Joan, 17 or 18, was going through difficult teenage years. Uncle Paul helped out with good advice.

Finally, the fifth son Jack (Page Gilman)—much younger than the rest—lived next door with his wife Betty. The big event of a few weeks before had been the birth of triplet girls: Abby, Debbie and Connie. The triplets joined three other girls in that family.

My relationship with the family became a regular Sunday afternoon tradition. My sisters listened, but I was the one who became the most fascinated. Summer brought changes. Most of the family moved to Claudia and Nicky's vacation home, the Sky Ranch. I pictured vast farmland and horses and many places to go. This was much more interesting than our own 400-acre farm in the Leaf Hills.

Many ordinary events took place too. Mother Barbour had a cold. A few years later, Father Barbour was teaching Margaret how to drive,

The Barbour family: Left to right, Claudia, Clifford, Mother Barbour, Paul, Hazel, Father Barbour and Jack.

and they ran out of gas on the Golden Gate Bridge, much to the annoyance of Father Barbour and the many drivers who were delayed.

In 1950, just as I finished eighth grade in our country school, the program moved from Sunday afternoon to each weekday evening at 6:45 (Central Time). I eagerly listened each evening during my high school years.

I was fascinated by Joan's life. One young man, a grease monkey at the airport, seemed like a nice young fellow, but Father Barbour did not feel this man was good enough for Joan. Another man became interested in her, but she was heartbroken when she discovered he was only interested in her because she would become a wealthy heiress.

On Christmas Day 1950, Joan married Ross Farnsworth. As it happened, her wedding closely followed the weddings of several of my own cousins.

I identified with Margaret because we were the same age and in the same grade. She seemed to have all the typical problems and concerns of a high school student. Then there was Claudia's daughter, Penelope, who became a first-rate jerk. Penelope, or "Penny," a thorn in Margaret's side, was just like some problem individuals in my own life.

When I left for college and later began a job teaching, I was not able to listen regularly to my story. The program moved from early evening to daytime. I missed my other family. During vacations and some other times, I managed to keep up with the Barbours.

My life was enriched because I knew this family. There were so many real elements. Mother Barbour grew older and became forgetful. Every Christmas the family would gather round the piano and she would play *Silent Night*. Then, Mother Barbour seemed to disappear from the scene. Some time later, her character returned, now played by Mary Adams. In 1951, Barton Yarborough, the actor who played Clifford, died. Clifford was written out of the

Mother and Father Barbour, 1946.

story: He went off to Scotland and married, never to return.

Father Barbour believed in the family and the permanence of marriage. When Joan and Ross had difficulties in their marriage and finally divorced, Father Barbour was devastated. He couldn't accept the divorce.

I ordered one of those premium books to get stories and pictures of the family. This book became my family album of the Barbours. I bought *Radio Mirror* for stories as well. I learned that *One Man's Family* was one of the most popular dramas on radio.

I learned also that the writer, Carlton E. Morse, felt that some of the problems of the time had come about because of the breakdown of the family. He wanted to create a story in which the family was strong. The Barbour family did remain strong, despite the differences and conflicts between generations and individuals.

The Barbours' story was real to me. People grew older, married, had children and died. This was life. That radio program had an intimacy that we don't find very often. Wouldn't it be great if we could have a radio or television family like this today?

My own family grew and changed too. There have been marriages and births and deaths and a host of changes. I have maintained close ties with my family. My grandmother lived until 1961, two years after the Barbour saga ended. My parents lived to be old—my mother lived past 100. Our family, or collection of families, still remains a strong institution. And *One Man's Family* showed us how to be a good family and the importance of family togetherness.

Families are important.

Unfortunately, I did not get to hear the final chapters of this great drama—really a series of novels rather than a soap opera. *One Man's Family* ended with Chapter 3,256, Book 136 on May 8, 1959.

What a wonderful influence it was in my life and in the lives of thousands of others! ❖

Radio's Most Popular Show

By Richard W. O'Donnell

Of all the shows to come on the radio since network radio was first established in the 1920s, which was the most popular? It wasn't Jack Benny, who was probably the airwaves' most famous star. Nor was it Orson Welles' *Mercury Theatre*, although his *War of the Worlds* drama has to be rated as the most famous individual radio program of all time.

If you said *Amos 'n' Andy*, radio's longest-running series, you are close, but not close enough. Not even the great Arthur Godfrey, who seemed to be on all the time, topped the list.

Easily the best-loved show of radio's glory days—the 1930s, '40s and early '50s—was *Fibber McGee and Molly*. The Tuesday-night favorite had the highest ratings in the land for most of its 18-year run.

Back then, Tuesday was the big night of the week in radio. Fibber and Molly were in good company on NBC on Tuesday nights, joining Bob Hope and Red Skelton. But the McGees were the cornerstone of NBC's most-listened-to night of radio. Fibber McGee and Molly ran a clean show with no double entendres allowed. It was a family show, and that's for sure.

The McGees were the cornerstone of NBC's most-listened-to night of radio.

For the record, Fibber and Molly McGee were played by a real-life married couple, Jim and Marian Jordan. The pair grew up in Peoria, Ill., and were high-school sweethearts. Once married, Jim tried a normal working life while his wife gave piano lessons at home.

In time, they decided show business was the life for them. While they enjoyed vaudeville, it kept them from their two young children, Kathryn and Jim Jr., so they settled in Chicago and tried radio. Once settled in the Windy City, they met Don Quinn, the writer who would pen most of their shows. With Quinn's help, they developed a show called *Smackout*, which was about a grocery store that was usually "smack out" of whatever the customers wanted.

When *Smackout* faded in the mid-1930s, the Jordans and Quinn came up with Fibber and Molly. The rest is radio history. Johnson Wax was looking for a show to sponsor nationally, and because Johnson was selling car wax, the McGees had most of their early adventures while traveling in an automobile.

Later, when Johnson decided to promote its new floor wax, the McGees found a house in a hurry! In fact, they won their celebrated abode at 79 Wistful Vista in a drawing. They quickly moved in, and they lived out their radio lives in that humble house. Needless to say, they always used Johnson Wax.

As the years passed, an endless parade of comic actors showed up at No. 79. They included Bill Thompson (The Old-Timer, Wallace Wimple and others); Gale Gordon (Mayor LaTrivia,); Cliff Arquette (The Old-Timer and Bessie); Arthur Q. Bryan (Doc Gamble); Mary Lou Croft (various roles); Bea Benaderet (Mrs. Carstairs); Marlin Hurt (Beulah); Dick LeGrand (Ole Swenson); Shirley Mitchell (Alice Darling); Isabel Randolph (Mrs. Uppington) and Hugh Studebaker (Silly Watson).

Jim and Marian Jordan,
the real-life Fibber McGee and Molly.

And who could forget Harold Peary as *The Great Gildersleeve*? He started out with the McGees, and then moved to Summerfield, where he had his own radio show for years. The Gildersleeve character, it is claimed, was the first "spin-off" on radio, and it set the stage for all those TV spin-offs we have today.

Don Quinn was the main writer. In fact, at the time, he was the highest paid writer on radio, and deservedly so.

He was later joined by Phil Leslie, who took charge when Quinn left the show to start Ronald Colman's radio show, *The Halls of Ivy*. Another writer, Keith Fowler, was a regular contributor to the show.

In 1937, two years after the show started its amazing run, Marian Jordan became ill. She was off the air for most of the 1937–38 season, returning only in June for a brief appearance as Teeny, the little girl who drove Fibber up a wall, and as Molly.

She assured the radio audience she would be back on a regular basis in the fall, when the show returned. And she was, but from time to time over the years, she would be off the air. The reason given for her absence was usually "family matters" or "personal business," and the actual illness was never made public. Most listeners never even suspected that Marian Jordan was ill.

The weekly *Fibber McGee and Molly* was dropped as a half-hour show in 1953. It came back in the fall as a five-times-a-week feature, and it lasted until 1957, when the McGees moved over to *Monitor*, a weekend NBC production, and did a series of short sketches.

Many of the most popular stars and shows of radio went on to equal success on television, but not Fibber and Molly. Because of her illness, Marian Jordan could not stand at a hanging microphone, as other performers did. For years, she had performed while sitting on stage at a table, all by herself. It would have been impossible to do a television show with a main character who was unable to move for any length of time.

NBC did try a series with comedian Bob Sweeney as Fibber and Cathy Lewis as Molly, but it lasted for only a few months in 1959. In 1960, NBC offered Marian and Jim Jordan a three-year contract to continue their sketches on *Monitor*. After serious discussion, they turned the offer down and retired from radio.

Marian Jordan passed away on April 6, 1961. Jim Jordan made a few radio appearances after that, and he appeared on a couple of TV shows. But radio was his medium, and television held no real appeal for him. He died on April 1, 1988.

Now the doorbell no longer chimes—and the closet door no longer opens, a signal for noisy calamity. ❖

BOB HOPE

Painted by

Norman Rockwell

On the Air With ...

Chapter Five

*I*f I had to choose my favorite personality from the airwaves in the Good Old Days, it would have to be that iconic figure in American entertainment, Bob Hope. Of course, my first introduction to Bob was on the silver screen in dozens of comedies.

He really hit his stride in the "Road" movies with Bing Crosby, taking us from Singapore to Zanzibar, to Morocco, to "Utopia," to Rio, to Bali and finally to Hong Kong. Those seven films spanned two decades and were more fun than a barrel of Bobs and Bings.

But it was in radio and television that Bob really proved his mettle. His first program on radio was the *Woodbury Soap Hour* on NBC in 1937. His show continued under different names denoting new sponsors for more than a decade before it was finally named what we were already calling it: *The Bob Hope Show*. He continued in radio until April 1955.

Some might think of Bob as the first cross-over artist. Well before radio began to wane as a medium for variety shows, Bob was already becoming a household name on the small screen. His first special programs for NBC-TV were aired in 1950.

One of my favorite stories of Bob's television escapades was from his appearance on *I Love Lucy* in 1956. When he received the script for the show, he reportedly said, "What? A script? I don't need one of these!" According to the legend, he then ad-libbed the entire episode. Lucille Ball and Desi Arnaz appeared later that year on one of Bob's TV specials.

> *Those seven films spanned two decades and were more fun than a barrel of Bobs and Bings.*

Bob was probably best known for two genres of special programs.

First, he was known as the perennial host of the Academy Awards programs. He always jousted with the Academy of Motion Picture Arts and Sciences because of the Academy's neglect in not selecting him for an Oscar.

In 1968, he opened the program: "Welcome to the Academy Awards, or as it's known at my house, Passover." In fact, while Bob was never nominated for an Academy Award, the AMPAS gave him four honorary awards, plus the Jean Hersholt Humanitarian Award in 1960.

Second, he was known for his Christmas specials. Who can forget those wonderful yuletide shows starring some of the most talented and charismatic entertainers of the 1960s and 1970s. He particularly was known for his Christmas USO specials filmed with and for servicemen and women in hotspots around the world. His 1970 and 1971 versions, filmed in Vietnam at the height of hostilities, were seen by more than 60 percent of U.S. households.

Bob turned 100 on May 29, 2003, and died less than two months later. But his legacy of love and laughter still refreshes me every time I queue up an old-time radio or TV program from my collection.

This chapter will give you personal glimpses into the lives of both the big and little stars of the Good Old Days. Go back on the air with those who, like Bob Hope, brought us all of those hours of joy on the airwaves in the Good Old Days.

—*Ken Tate*

Memories From a Golden Age

By Marilou Putman as told to Christine Venzon

I love old movies, especially the ones about the talented but innocent ingenue who leaves her small town in the Midwest to find fame and fortune in the theater. You see, I lived that script, although the ending isn't one Hollywood would have written. I grew up in Council Bluffs, Iowa, in the 1920s. My father ran a hotel, which he built himself. He loved the theater and music. I remember him always singing. Sadly, he died when I was 9 years old, leaving us three women—my mother, my younger sister Kay, and me—to fend for ourselves.

As I got older, I took my responsibility to help support my family very seriously. And my father had left me a way to do that: his love for theater. I didn't "follow my star" to Broadway. I followed it to Duchesne College of the Sacred Heart, just across the river in Omaha, Neb., where I got a drama scholarship. I worked hard there to learn the skills and the craft, to be professional. The drama director thought I had some talent and set up auditions for me with NBC, ABC and CBS—the "big three of radio—in Chicago.

———— *✦✦✦* ————

The drama director thought I had some talent and set up auditions for me in Chicago.

———— *✦✦✦* ————

For two months I made the rounds, getting to know radio people and the all-important sponsors. Radio shows were as much advertisement for the company that sponsored them as they were entertainment for the audience. Talent didn't count for much if the sponsor didn't think you fit their image.

In Chicago I met Alan Wallace, who was directing *Little Orphan Annie* for Ovaltine, the chocolate-drink maker. They were looking for a more exciting image, and they had started sponsoring *Captain Midnight*, an adventure serial about a crime-fighting pilot.

Alan was impressed by my background in what he called "legitimate theater." He asked me to audition for a new character in the show: Joyce Ryan, a flyer in Captain Midnight's Secret Squadron. The audition was three hours long, and I was up against about 50 other women. But I got the part.

I played Joyce Ryan for the next six years, from about 1940 to 1946. The role rekindled another interest I inherited from my father:

Facing page: The author (right) performs on Captain Midnight *with Jack Bivens (left) and Ed Prentiss (center) in September 1943.*

flying. I earned my pilot's license while working on the show (although, unlike Joyce, I never flew raids against the Nazis).

My contract had me working on *Captain Midnight* four days a week, and I always worked a fifth day if needed. It paid well, about $350 a week. I could also take any other job that didn't conflict with the show. That left me the whole morning and a lot of nights to fill. That's when all that work in college paid off, especially the voice training. I could do the high-up voice of a little girl or the low sultry voice of the femme fatale.

At one point, I was doing four programs a day. One of them was *The First Nighter*. The show featured original dramas broadcast from an imaginary "little theater off Times Square." In reality, it was the Merchandise Mart in Chicago, but the sound effects had you believing you were walking along a Broadway street and into the theater just before the curtain rose. It was radio drama at its best. And it was a plum for an up-and-coming actress. I was playing alongside Hugh Downs, Mike Wallace and even Orson Welles.

Also, I was earning enough money to move my mother and sister to Chicago. I found us a place up on the North Side, a nice apartment right on the lake. I put my sister in a very good Catholic school.

Then came my big break—almost. After I did a show for NBC in California, Paramount offered me a film contract—not as a leading lady, but as part of their "stable." That was the way the studios operated then. They paid you a pittance just to be sure you were available if they needed an extra or a bit player. Sometimes you made the leap to stardom, but I didn't have any illusions about my chances. I was a talented, professional actress for radio. But for the big screen, I had the wrong kind of teeth, the wrong kind of hair, the wrong kind of everything—so I said no.

That didn't stop me from finding my leading man. He wasn't someone Hollywood would cast. He was a medical resident at the Mayo Clinic, a small fellow with the unlikely name of Harrison Putman (and an unlikelier nickname, "Put"). He was a friend of my steady date at the time, Bill Lightner. One evening, the three of us went to dinner. Bill begged off early. They had spent the day at the lake, and he was terribly ill with a bad sunburn. Put drove me home, and we sat and talked until 4 in the morning. Two weeks later, we were engaged. (Now *that's* a whirlwind romance worthy of Hollywood.)

That's where I wrote "The End" to my career. As I promised, I gave up all my radio roles for the role of wife and mother. And those parts were more challenging than any radio drama—but that's another story. Through it all, I have been very fortunate. The good Lord has been with me when I needed Him—in those days, the Good Old Days of radio's golden age, and beyond. ❖

Above: A Captain Midnight *decoder badge from 1946, the author's last year with the program.*
Facing page: The author with an unnamed soldier at an Army base during World War II.

Me and the Captain

By Brenda McGuire Hicks as told to Donna McGuire Tanner

Even though I was only 5 years old at the time, I remember it as if it happened this morning. It was Monday, Oct. 3, 1955, a crisp, cool fall day at my home on a hill in Weirwood, W. Va. My older brother, Danny, and sister, Donna, had just left to run down the hill to catch the school bus. My mother, Rachel, was washing breakfast dishes in the kitchen while little brother Jackie entertained himself with his toy cars. My 2-month-old baby brother, Randy, was asleep in his crib, and my father, Basil, was fast asleep too, after working the night shift in the coal mine.

I felt so alone with no one around, so I went to the black-and-white Admiral television in the corner and snapped it on. It took a minute or so to warm up. I could hear the happy music before I could see the picture. I did not recognize the man with the heavy mustache and the strange cap. He wore a coat with oversized pockets. Then, in his soft-spoken voice, he introduced himself as Captain Kangaroo. *So that is why he has big pockets!* I thought to myself.

> *One of my favorite parts of the program was when Mr. Green Jeans stopped by for a visit.*

When the Captain took out his keys to enter the "Treasure House," he opened a whole new world for me. In this place dwelled many make-believe inhabitants.

Mr. Moose was a puppet, but he just didn't realize it. He always had a knock-knock joke that ended with hundreds of Ping-Pong balls falling on the Captain's head.

The Dancing Bear, which looked like an oversized teddy bear, seemed to be there most of the time. And bespectacled Bunny Rabbit made his daily appearance, using his trickery to get a bunch of carrots.

One of my favorite parts of the program was when Mr. Green Jeans (played by Hugh "Lumpy" Brannum) stopped by for a visit. In this pre-color television era, I could only imagine that he had been given that name because he wore green bib overalls. He usually wore a straw hat, which made me think he was a farmer. Mr. Green Jeans brought animals to visit the Captain. This gave me a lifelong respect and love for animals.

Guest stars visited the Treasure House too; I remember Carol Channing and Imogene Coca. Most were in character, though, so I did not recognize many of them.

Cartoons were part of the *Captain Kangaroo* experience. The one I recall was *Tom Terrific*. Music and songs, such as *Big Rock*

Facing page: Bob Keeshan as Captain Kangaroo (driving a bus with a pot cover for a steering wheel) with Hugh "Lumpy" Brannum as Mr. Green Jeans. (Photo by Lisa Larsen// Time Life Pictures/Getty Images)

Candy Mountain, were incorporated into the program too.

Every day, in hushed tones, the Captain would tell us kids who were watching that it was time to wake Grandfather Clock. Grandfather always had his eyes closed tight. When the Captain told us, we were supposed to shout, "Wake up, Grandfather!" I had to be mindful that my dad was still asleep, and so was baby Randy. But I did say it. And Grandfather's eyes always snapped open.

I suppose the reason I was so taken with this program is that they kept it simple, and I always felt that they were doing it just for me.

After watching *Captain Kangaroo* that first day, I could not wait for my sister to get home from school. I tried to explain it to her, but she could not catch my excitement. I just knew she would have to wait until she could see it herself.

What I did not realize at the time was that Captain Kangaroo was already an old friend. He had once played Clarabelle the Clown on

Two children's favorites—Mr. Rogers and Captain Kangaroo share the stage on an episode of Captain Kangaroo *in 1970. Mr. Rogers (Fred Rogers, 1928–2003) was a guest of Captain Kangaroo (Bob Keeshan, 1927–2004). Rogers wears his trademark blue V-neck sweater and rests his hands on a gramophone horn; Keeshan wears his "captain's" uniform—a red blazer with white piping. (Photo by CBS Photo Archive/Getty Images)*

the *Howdy Doody* program. Now, unmasked and minus his fake mustache, he was humanly known as Bob Keeshan.

The program proved to be so popular with kids that after only about three months, CBS extended it from a five-day-a-week, hour-long program to six days, including Saturdays. Finally, we sisters could watch it together—and when it was time to wake Grandfather Clock, our parents gave us permission to shout because our father was already awake and enjoying a leisurely Saturday-morning breakfast.

Time passed, and as I grew older, the Captain faded into memory. Then, when my first child, Johnny, was in his pre-walking stage,

we watched *Captain Kangaroo* together. Soon, he would awaken everyone early in the morning by shouting "Roo-roo!" Like Grandfather Clock, it was a signal that it was time for me to awaken.

Again, time slipped away. Before I knew it, my children were grown. One day I was channel switching—by this time, I had a color television set, and many stations from which to choose. Suddenly, there was my old friend! How sad I was that there were no children with me to watch.

I found myself laughing at the same characters from my childhood. I realized that the past had met the present. Once more it was just me and the Captain. ❖

Good Morning, Captain!

By Glen Herndon

*I*n those Good Old Days, true happiness for my little girls was a fresh bowl of hot buttered popcorn and a visit with Captain Kangaroo. And fresh new dresses Mother had made them for church guaranteed happy smiles.

We lived then in a suburb of Detroit, and our television was only a cheap black-and-white. With only rabbit ears for an antenna, reception was always poor—and it took a lot of patience to enjoy anything on it. But that mattered not a whit to those precious little girls on that sunny morning in 1960 when I photographed them enjoying a visit from their television grandpa.

Truth be told, Bob Keeshan was only a year older than their 32-year-old daddy. But the calm persona he created influenced millions of youngsters for the good. I rarely got to see his program, but I remember well that day his sidekick, Mr. Green Jeans, was feeding carrots to a little goat and telling quietly about goats in an entertaining manner. The Captain was busy that day trying to cure Mr. Moose and Bunny Rabbit of their naughty ways.

Other days I would come home to find my girls doing some little project the Captain had suggested. And he kept his show going for an astounding 38 years, from 1955–1993! We were saddened when we heard of his death. His wholesome influence on millions was incalculable. ❖

The author's daughters (left to right), Nancy, Janice and Michele, enjoy their favorite television program.

Half a Century With Bergen and McCarthy

By Roy Meador

Charlie was right. There's no doubt about it; when he pulled the strings and made the wooden dummy talk, the ventriloquist's lips moved. He made no particular effort to hide the fact when you saw him in person or on the screen. He always seemed apologetic, bumbling and a little clumsy, at least in comparison with the frank, feisty and ferocious Charlie.

But these little drawbacks just didn't seem to matter. On radio, you couldn't see the ventriloquist anyway, and so what if his lips moved? What came out of those lips was what really counted. In the artful business of making people laugh and feel good, he was unbeatable. He was Edgar Bergen, and on his knee was Charlie McCarthy.

America's love affair with Bergen and McCarthy began on May 9, 1937, when radio's *The Chase and Sanborn Hour* introduced the odd but irresistible entertainers to a national audience on a weekly basis. *The Edgar Bergen and Charlie McCarthy Show* is what it was, even though it used another name for a time.

> *Doubts that radio and ventriloquism wouldn't mix were totally routed by the results of Dec. 17, 1936.*

Bergen and McCarthy rapidly zoomed to the top in radio popularity and handily held the summit against all competition for several years. Sunday night at 8 p.m. with Edgar and Charlie became a formidable and established national habit, like Sunday papers, morning coffee and summer baseball. "Did you hear what Charlie said last night?" was a much-repeated Monday-morning question across the land, and that alone was usually sufficient to bring on shared laughter. Charlie had a way of saying what no one else had the nerve to say, and somehow you treasured him all the more for his frank, debonair and incorrigible observations.

Easily and inevitably, listeners forgot that Charlie wasn't actually alive. They forgot that his bold, wicked comments were actually Bergen speaking through the painted wooden lips. We wanted Charlie to be alive, so we insisted, pretended and believed that he was.

Analyzing the strange, powerful impact of Charlie McCarthy on the nation in 1939, *The New York Times* reported: "Psychologists say that Charlie differs from other dummies because he has definite

American ventriloquist and comedian Edgar Bergen, flanked by his dummies Mortimer Snerd (right) and Charlie McCarthy, with his daughter, future actress Candice Bergen, playing the piano. (Photo by Tom Kelley/Hulton Archive/Getty Images)

spiritual qualities. His throaty, almost lecherous chuckle is a haunting thing; his whole attitude of *Weltschmerz* is astonishingly real. He says things that a human actor never would dare to say in public and get away with them."

Even Bergen seemed to believe—or at least go along with—the general feeling that Charlie was much more than simply a ventriloquist's tool. He insured the original Charlie for $10,000 and named him as a beneficiary in his will. Bergen stood quietly by when Charlie took the limelight, received honorary degrees from universities and became engaged to Marilyn Monroe on the radio show. Articles even claimed that Bergen was jealous of Charlie's popularity, gregarious nature and facility in making friends.

No doubt Edgar Bergen cried all the way to the bank. By the mid-1940s, in the company of Charlie McCarthy, Bergen's take-home pay from the radio show was nearly $10,000 a week. Charlie McCarthy collectibles and memorabilia—dolls, toys and mementos—earned the team another $100,000 each year. And Charlie, content to get most of the laughs and hog center stage as top banana, generously let Bergen have all the money.

Before their success on network radio, sparring microphone to microphone with W.C. Fields, John Barrymore and other great entertainers, Edgar Bergen and Charlie McCarthy put in long and arduous years learning what makes people laugh and how to stimulate the process.

Born Feb. 16, 1903, and raised on a Michigan farm, Edgar Bergen studied ventriloquism as a boy. He discovered early on that he could entertain people by pretending to throw his voice and saying funny things unexpectedly. It soon turned out that he had a special gift for saying funny things.

As a youth, he used money he had earned to hire a woodcarver to carve the original Charlie from white pine. The head with movable jaws was attached to a stick, and the whole ensemble was outfitted in garments. The model for the head was a Decatur newspaper hawker named Charlie. The woodcarver was Theodore Mack. Edgar Bergen logically named his new companion Charlie McCarthy. It was an easy and inspired way to recognize the contributions Charlie and Mr. Mack made to the historic effort.

During the 1920s, Bergen and McCarthy wandered the world, lived out of (and in) a trunk, entertaining wherever and whomever they could. They learned, improved and steadily progressed, finding work at first in the lower echelons of vaudeville. Eventually, their struggles earned them admittance into the big time. In 1930 they reached the top of vaudeville's Everest by appearing at the world's entertainment capital: the Palace Theatre, Broadway and 47th Street, New York City.

Charlie McCarthy and Edgar Bergen photo,
House of White Birches nostalgia archives

Finally secure in the vaudeville stratosphere, Bergen saw the whole tinsel structure swiftly collapse and fade. The Palace closed in 1932, and vaudeville gave up the ghost as radio and movies took over entertaining a nation. Like the village blacksmith when automobiles replaced the horse, Bergen had to seek new audiences and sources of income. Charlie's appetite was meager, but human actors had to eat.

Bergen changed his act by putting Charlie in a fancy dress suit and giving him a monocle. He wrote a new act suitable for nightclubs. One notable amendment was making Charlie bolder, sharper and faster with a cutting quip. In the act,

Charlie informed Bergen that he belonged behind a plow back on the farm, and that the people in the audience would be complimented no matter what he called them. Charlie became a clown prince of insult, and the act was a smash.

Success at New York's Rainbow Room brought Bergman an invitation to perform on Rudy Vallee's Thursday-night radio variety show, *The Fleischmann Hour*. Any doubts that radio and ventriloquism wouldn't mix were totally routed by the results of Dec. 17, 1936. Bergen and McCarthy delighted the listeners, and Vallee brought them back several times.

Chase and Sanborn concluded that such merriment would help sell coffee. Edgar Bergen and Charlie McCarthy soon had their own show, and practically overnight, they eclipsed the prominence they had achieved with such difficulty in vaudeville. Network radio made them a cherished and permanent national institution as America's Sunday-night dials were tuned to the Edgar and Charlie show.

To set up new situations and expanded program possibilities, Bergen created dimwitted-but-amiable Mortimer Snerd, man-hungry Effie Klinker and preposterous Podine Puffington. Mortimer especially pleased audiences with his cheerful modesty. "Just lucky, I guess," he replied when Bergen asked how he could be so stupid. But these competitors had no real effect on Charlie's sovereignty. The immodest, sarcastic, unscrupulous, undaunted Charlie McCarthy ruled Bergen's dummy trunk—and the American airwaves.

Edgar Bergen and Charlie McCarthy continued on radio until 1956. Through the years, they appeared in films as well. The film they made with their old friend and adversary W.C. Fields, *You Can't Cheat an Honest Man*, is a classic of 20th century American comedy.

Following their radio years, Bergen and McCarthy continued to work much as they had in the early days, traveling from engagement to engagement, club to club, benefit to benefit. They worked political conventions, fairs, television and nightclubs. It was different in their later years of trunk-and-suitcase entertaining,

however; now they were known and loved wherever they appeared. In their own time, Edgar Bergen and Charlie McCarthy were recognized as performers for the ages.

In 1978 Bergen announced his retirement and booked a final three-week appearance at Caesar's Palace in Las Vegas. He shared the bill with Andy Williams. With the theme song *Charlie My Boy* playing, Bergen and McCarthy took the stage and earned a standing ovation from the capacity crowd of fans and show-business greats.

The old partners appeared for three nights in succession, sharing the familiar jokes with affectionate and appreciative audiences. Bergen ended his farewell performances by saying, "In vaudeville, every act has to have an opening and a close, and I think for me, the close has come, and it's time to pack up my little friends and say goodbye."

> *Charlie, content getting the laughs and hogging center stage, generously let Bergen have all the money.*

The morning after the third performance, Edgar Bergen was found permanently asleep in his hotel suite. The act was ended.

At the end of a play, Ethel Barrymore once said, "That's all there is, there isn't any more." Fortunately, this could not be said about Edgar Bergen and Charlie McCarthy. The great journey they had made together for nearly 60 years will never be finished as long as the human race needs laughter as nourishment for life.

Ronald Reagan, in a funeral eulogy for Edgar Bergen, said, "He was a puckish, pixie-like destroyer of the pompous." Johnny Carson called him the most unpretentious man he had ever met. Charlie McCarthy appropriately was put on display at the Smithsonian Institution in the nation's capital.

We still hear them clearly, ventriloquist Bergen and his smart-aleck little chum, McCarthy. We hear Bergen remonstrating with Charlie and soothing his ruffled feathers. We hear Charlie indignantly declaring, "I'll mow you down, so help me, I'll mow you down!"

Mow ahead, Charlie McCarthy. We love it and you. And we thank the man, Edgar Bergen, whose lips moved visibly while saying wonderfully funny things. ❖

I Remember Olivio Santoro

By Rowena Stuart

Some people recall a friend or family member from childhood—someone who has left a special mark on their memory. For me, that person was an entertainer on a children's radio program. It was sometime in the late 1930s in New York City, and I must have been 7 or 8 when my mother discovered the program. She was delighted—anything to get me out of bed on a weekend morning.

The program was *The Horn & Hardart Children's Hour*, and one of the entertainers was known as "Olivio Santoro, the Boy Yodeler." He strummed a guitar, sang and yodeled. And I was mesmerized. *Surely he is singing just for me*, I thought, sitting in front of our floor-model Zenith. He seemed so close. I imagined him actually living somewhere inside the radio.

The program featured many children, including the Moylan Sisters, Peggy Joan and Marianne. The theme song for the program was *Less Work for Mother*, meaning that eating at the Horn & Hardart Automat (the sponsor), with its excellent food and low prices, indeed meant "less work for Mother."

> ### He strummed a guitar, sang and yodeled. And I was mesmerized.

I had visited the automat many times. I always marveled at the lightning speed with which they made change for a dollar with nickels that seemed to come swooping out. Then I'd deposit those nickels into the wall machines, all lined up with delicious-looking food.

Sometimes I wondered if I might run into Olivio Santoro there, but I had no idea what he looked like. Years later, I learned that if my mother had written and requested a picture, they would have sent one.

I listened to *The Horn & Hardart Children's Hour* for years. I soon discovered that Olivio Santoro also had his own 15-minute program sponsored by Philadelphia Scrapple, a cereal-and-pork concoction. Olivio sang that theme song.

When I was older, I wanted to find out more about my childhood idol. In the process, I gathered information from his sister, his wife, and even from Olivio himself via mail and phone.

His mom and dad came to this country from Italy and settled in New York, where they raised six children—four boys and two girls.

During his growing-up years in Inwood, Long Island, he met many famous people, including Arthur Godfrey, Gene Autry, Roy Rogers and others, and says he was thrilled to "hang out" with Elton Britt. He also had his own horse.

Olivio's interest in country music began when he was 6 years old. His idol then was a singer-yodeler named Montana Slim (Wilf Carter), whom he heard on local radio.

Olivio made his own first guitar. "I took a cigar box, made a hole in the center, attached rubber bands to it, and sang and yodeled my heart away. I thought I was Elton Britt and Montana Slim all in one."

Olivio was quite young when he was "discovered." His dad was in the landscape business, and his customers included the parents of actor Paul Stewart. When they heard the young yodeler, Stewart, a well-known announcer at NBC, suggested that Olivio audition for *The Horn & Hardart Children's Hour*. Olivio's musical talents won them over, and soon he was performing regularly.

Later he had his own show. He remembers that day in 1941 when, while he was doing the show, a news flash came on announcing that Pearl Harbor had just been bombed.

His producers were working on a movie for him with Gene Autry, but before that happened, he left to go into the Navy. After his discharge in 1946, he appeared on Arthur Godfrey's show and also had his own TV show called *Friendship Ranch*. "What a thrill," he says. "Every Thursday night, 6 to 6:30 p.m." He also appeared on *Howdy Doody* with Buffalo Bob.

Looking back, he says his show-business career was fun. He eventually went into the family landscape business.

In retirement, Olivio Santoro lives in New York with his wife. They are parents of a son and daughter and several grandchildren. According to his wife, Olivio still performs—but only for family.

Thanks to Olivio Santoro, I developed a lifelong appreciation of country-and-western and bluegrass music. And I sincerely thank him.

I'd give anything to once more hear my mother calling out on a weekend morning, "Hurry, get out of bed! Olivio Santoro is coming on. You don't want to miss him now, do you?" No indeed, I didn't. ❖

Olivio Santoro strumming, singing and yodeling.

Frank and Dr. I.Q.

By Richard W. O'Donnell

Every time I watch one of those television shows where they give away thousands of dollars, my memory harkens back to 1942, when I almost was on the *Dr. I.Q.* radio show. They chose the guy in the next seat. *Dr. I.Q.*, "the Mental Banker," was a quiz show on NBC from 1939–1948, and the year after that on ABC.

What made this show different was that it was a traveling quiz show. It stayed for seven weeks at a major theater in a big city, and then moved on to another location.

Every other year, *Dr. I.Q.* came to the Metropolitan Theater in Boston, where I grew up. Every time it did, I talked my older brother Frank into taking me to one of the Monday-night movies. *Dr. I.Q.* came on after the second feature and before the main attraction. Nine announcers hired from local radio shows were situated throughout the theater, where they could select members of the audience and allow them to answer a question.

Several hosts filled the roll of Dr. I.Q. On the night I recall, Jim McClain was in charge.

Contestants won silver dollars for answering questions correctly—$5 for an easy one, $10 for a more difficult one, and so on, up to $20.

Then there was the weekly biography. You started up around $50 and worked your way down. Every time you missed a clue, you lost dough, until all your money was gone.

Losers were given a package of Mars bars. Mars sponsored the show during most of its run. The consolation prize was almost as good as winning five silver dollars.

"I have a lady in the balcony," an announcer in the theater would call out. Her name would be given, and perhaps her occupation and local town. Then Dr. I.Q. would ask, "For five silver dollars, what type of pet did Mary have?"

Once the question was answered, another announcer took over. "John W. Twerp is with us tonight, Dr. I.Q. He's an elevator operator."

And Dr. I.Q. would fire back, "For 10 silver dollars, how many white stripes are in the American flag?" When the answer was given, it was on to the next question. This continued nonstop, except for the commercials.

On our night of nights, I was waving, trying to get the announcer's attention. But he ignored me. I was too young, I guess. Instead, he chose the guy next to me—my brother, Frank.

"You want to go on?" asked the announcer. Frank hadn't been waving. But he replied, "Why not?" And lo and behold, it was the big one! It was the biography.

> *Losers were given a package of Mars bars.*

Dr. I.Q. came up with the first clue. "This famous American writer was born in Boston in 1809. Who is he?"

Almost as soon as the question was asked, Frank fired back, "Edgar Allan Poe!"

My brother was right! He was the deep one in the family, always listening to classical music and reading books by 19th-century authors.

"You've won 50 silver dollars!" Dr. I.Q. shouted happily. "Congratulations!"

The audience went wild, cheering and applauding as the show went to commercial.

They gave my brother his prize that night. He didn't actually receive silver dollars. Can you imagine lugging all that heavy dough home late at night in Boston back then? I think they gave him the green stuff; it didn't weigh as much.

Later, my brother gave me $10. "I wouldn't have gone to that show if you hadn't dragged me there," Frank stated. "You deserve a share of the prize." In those days, a ten-spot was a small fortune. I was rich—but only for a few days.

Dr. I.Q. is only a fond memory now. They tried him on television for a while, but he didn't work out. He's been off the air for decades, but I'll never forget the good doctor. ❖

Unforgettable "Noncelebrities"

By Jim McClain (aka Dr. I.Q.)

*L*ooking back over the many years since first I saw the light of day, I realize that I have met a greater number of interesting and famous persons than the average guy. It has occurred to me, however, that some of the most interesting people I have known were not famous celebrities at all. They were little-known men and women doing their work and living their lives with no fanfare or spotlight. I'd like to tell you about some of these "noncelebrities" who are indelibly etched on my memory.

Take Morris "Speck" Brownlee, for instance. He was my first boss—an insurance man who unselfishly launched me on a career that took me away from his business and gave me my first job in broadcasting.

It was 1934. America was in the middle of the worst economic depression this nation had ever seen. I was 22, recently married and looking for a job. My clergyman introduced me to his friend, Morris "Speck" Brownlee, a life insurance agent.

Speck gave me a job selling life insurance—that is, *trying* to sell life insurance. I received a draw against future commissions from my sales. The problem was that I made no sales.

Not that I didn't try. For months, I called on prospects, worked up prospectus plans, pleaded for appointments—all to no avail. I knew too little about insurance and nothing at all about how to sell it. Meanwhile, I was drawing money for living expenses, and the account was building higher and higher.

After several months of futility, Speck saw that I was ready to throw in the sponge. He suggested I try something else. "You were good at debating and acting in college, Jim. Why not get a job in broadcasting?"

I told him that this would be difficult to do with trained announcers out of work all over the country. But he insisted that I visit the local radio station and audition for a friend of his who was the program director.

With little hope, I applied. Imagine my surprise when I was hired! The program director said he would pay me a small salary as a student announcer until I could learn the ropes. It was enough for my wife and me to live on, and it

was certainly preferable to the drawing account that was driving us deeper and deeper into debt.

Brownlee was delighted when I returned with the good news. "I knew you could do it, Jim. Don't worry about the drawing account debt. Someday you can pay it back when you're making a lot of money."

Several months later, the station made me a regular full-time member of the staff with a full-time salary. We began making payments on the drawing account.

It was not until 10 years later, after I had become successful as Dr. I.Q. on the NBC network, that I learned the whole truth of that first job. Speck Brownlee had called the program director before my arrival and had asked him to give me a chance to prove myself. He arranged to pay my salary himself for as long as it took for me to learn the job. All during those months when I was a "student announcer" at WFAA, Dallas, Brownlee was secretly reimbursing the station for my weekly salary.

I learned also that he helped many other young people get a start in life, acting on his faith in his fellow man and in the American system of free enterprise.

Even in retirement, Speck continued to contribute generously to young people who needed a boost in starting their careers.

Another unforgettable noncelebrity who played a large part in my career was an advertising man named Will C. Grant. He hired me in 1939 to be radio director of his Dallas agency. Within a few months, I was promoted and moved to his Chicago headquarters, where I was given the task of producing and directing a new show on the NBC Blue Network. The show was *What's Your Idea?*, and it was an incredible headache.

We offered cash prizes each week to lis-

teners who submitted original ideas for new radio programs. With three winners each week, it was my job to build 10-minute vignettes to showcase the winning ideas, all within the framework of a half-hour show. I had an orchestra, a stable of actors, a writer and a famous guest star each week.

The show was a momentous fiasco—a bomb—a real turkey! The ratings were so bad that we were lucky to get through the original 13-week contract. None of us was surprised when *What's Your Idea?* expired.

Mars *Dr. I.Q.* ad, House of White Birches nostalgia archives

But Will Grant was not discouraged. Even though I had engineered a colossal flop, he didn't hold it against me. In fact, he suggested that I go back to the Dallas office and "take it easy" for a while until I had recovered from the shock of failure. Then, no sooner had I arrived in Texas than he called me to say that his *Dr. I.Q. Show* needed a new Dr. I.Q. It seemed that the man who was enacting the role had fallen from favor with the sponsors and had to be replaced. I was drafted and flown to Seattle to take over the show. I went from a total failure to a nation-

ally known celebrity in the space of 24 hours! It was the sort of thing Will C. Grant was especially good at—pulling strings, manipulating people, turning tragedy into triumph. Nobody in the world did it quite so neatly as Will C. Grant.

Grant was a soft-spoken Texan with an easy drawl, and a set of goals and ambitions that stopped just short of becoming president of the United States. A total stranger to Chicago, without a single national account, and with only a few dollars in his pocket, Grant had barged into the executive offices of Mars Inc., the candy bar company, and informed the astonished advertising manager that he knew exactly what was wrong with the company's advertising, and that his agency had an infallible plan for making

Mars candy the best-selling candy bar in the world. At the time, Milky Way was far down the list of best-sellers.

The ad manager was so amused by Grant's audacity that he decided to listen. After an hour, he became convinced that this profoundly charming Texan had a lot to offer.

Like most great ideas, Grant's was a simple one. "Instead of constant reminders of quality ingredients, spotless government-inspected kitchens and fine-quality chocolate, eggs, milk and sugar," Grant insisted that all the consumer was interested in was the taste. He argued, "You have to make the customer taste that candy! Describe the flavor! Make the consumer so hungry for that candy bar that he'll do most anything to get one!"

An hour later, Grant walked out of that office with the Mars account in his pocket. An unknown advertising genius from Texas had wrapped up his first million-dollar account. Six months later, Milky Way was the fastest-selling candy bar in the country and Mars Inc. was on top.

There have been other interesting non-celebrities whose paths crossed mine. I always enjoy looking back at these incredible characters and the role each played in the world Shakespeare insisted was but a stage. ❖

Remembering Schnozzola

By Mario DeMarco

Jimmy Durante wasn't a big man in stature, but once he was on the stage, he transformed himself by taking charge of the hall, playing, singing, doing a dance or two, and cracking jokes. There was only one like him—he was a product of the stage and the Bowery; if the audience there didn't care for a performer's routine, they let him know immediately. Jimmy was brought up in this show-business atmosphere, and he called it home.

Jimmy's given name was James Francis Durante, and he was born on Feb. 10, 1893, in New York City. He was the son of a fast-talking sideshow barker. Jimmy's oversize nose earned him the nickname "Schnozzola," but it actually enhanced his entertainment career rather than discouraged it.

He was only 16 years old when he began playing ragtime piano with his partners Lou Clayton and Eddie Jackson. It wasn't long before the trio's act clicked with audiences, and they played in nightclubs and on vaudeville circuits. Their big chance came in 1929 when they were contracted to perform on Broadway, at the New York Palace, where they were featured in Ziegfeld's highly successful show, *Show Girl*.

The following year, Hollywood beckoned. MGM handed him a five-year movie contract. In the following years, Durante both played on Broadway and was committed to Hollywood for film work—and he was a star in both media. Some of Jimmy's most memorable movies include *The Cuban Love Song*; *Little Miss Broadway*; *The Man Who Came to Dinner*; *Jumbo;* and *It's a Mad, Mad, Mad, Mad World*.

There was one goal left to conquer: radio. There, too, his act soon had the listeners under his spell. As a master comic, he made good use of his hoarse singing voice; and yet, he could also bring tears to his audience's eyes.

When television entered the realm of entertainment, Jimmy was again welcomed with open arms by the fans.

His great career in entertainment lasted more than 40 years. Those who were fortunate enough to see him in person on the stage, hear him on radio, or catch his act in movies, on television or in Las Vegas laughed and laughed. He always left the audience feeling good. And when he left them, this outstanding all-around comic always signed off with his trademark phrase: "Good night, Mrs. Calabash, wherever you are!" ❖

Art Carney

By Joseph Curreri

As lovable, floppy Ed Norton on *The Honeymooners*, Art Carney made sewer workers happy. In *Harry and Tonto*, he made cat lovers happy. In *Happy Endings*, he played a pantomime, keeping his mouth shut—"which made many people happy," joked Carney. Then he kept senior citizens happy by playing lovable old codgers. But it was as Jackie Gleason's bumbling sidekick, Ed Norton, as part of the greatest TV comedy team of all time, that he made millions of people happy—and he still does!

Tracing Art Carney's life from childhood, through struggles with alcoholism and depression, his prolific work in theater, TV and films, to his death at age 85 on Nov. 9, 2003, peels away his second-banana image. What's left is an accomplished actor who earned six Emmys and an Oscar (for best actor, in the 1974 film *Harry and Tonto*).

> *"Before I started doing Norton, I always was very shy. The character changed me."*

After 37 years in the acting business, at age 55, he finally got a starring role in a movie. In *Harry and Tonto*, he played a sprightly 72-year-old who refused to relinquish his relish for life.

"I got top billing—over a cat," Carney said. "But that was my first big break in films. Just proves that life is available to anyone, no matter what age. All you have to do is grab it.

"You know what Jackie Gleason did when I won the Oscar? He called me at 6 o'clock the next morning when I was still in bed. He talked to me for 20 minutes."

Winning an Oscar always prompts a deluge of movie offers. Carney played older men in a string of movies, notably *Going in Style* with George Burns, a 1980 film about three old men who rob a bank; *The Undergrads*, in which he rode a motorcycle and attended college with his grandson; *A Doctor's Story* (1984) and *Terrible Joe Moran* (1984) with James Cagney.

"I was swamped with George Stone and Charlie Pickford parts—old men," Carney said. "But I like to work. When you work hard and have fun, it's not work anymore. I hate to gift-wrap garbage—that's what I do when I don't work."

Still, the character the world will always remember is Art Carney's Ed Norton of *The Honeymooners*—rubber-limbed in T-shirt and vest, dumpy hat askew.

Facing page: Jackie Gleason, Art Carney, Joyce Randoph and Audrey Meadows stand by a bannerannouncing a raffle for a new TV on the set of the television series,The Honeymooners, circa 1956. Photo by Paramount Television, Getty Images

Jackie Gleason comes up with another hairbrained scheme while Art Carney, Audrey Meadows and Joyce Randoph listen in disbelief on the television series, The Honeymooners, circa 1956. Photo courtesy the author

Arthur William Matthew Carney was born Nov. 4, 1918, in Mount Vernon, a New York City suburb. His father was a newspaperman, his mother a former concert violinist.

"I always wanted to be a jazz pianist," he said, "but I didn't study very hard and wound up playing by ear."

As a youngster, he had a talent for mimicry, entertaining family and friends by imitating famous voices he heard on radio. In 1936, at 18, he got a job as a mimic with Horace Heidt's Orchestra. Traveling with Heidt, Art missed slim, blond Jean Myers, his Mount Vernon sweetheart. In 1940, they were married.

The Heidt Band introduced him to the bottle. Alcoholism and depression would plague him for more than 30 years thereafter.

Drafted into the Army, Art was wounded in France in July 1944. For the next five years, he worked on radio, mostly as a stooge for comedians like Morey Amsterdam and Robert Q. Lewis.

In 1950 he auditioned for Gleason, and Ed Norton emerged to delight at least two generations of television viewers. In 1953, 1954 and 1955, Carney became the first actor to win three consecutive Emmy awards! He also appeared in all 39 episodes when *The Honeymooners* aired as a series in 1955–1956. Years later, these episodes were big sellers in video stores and on DVDs.

His private life was less successful. He had originated the Broadway role of Felix Unger in *The Odd Couple* in 1965, playing opposite Walter Matthau, but he couldn't keep up. He quit and checked himself into a hospital. His marriage to Jean came apart after three children. He later married Barbara Isaac, and after they divorced, he remarried Jean. This time, their union held firm.

Gleason brought him out of the hospital to do a *Honeymooners Special* on his CBS series. It was such a hit that a revived *Honeymooners*, with Sheila MacRae as Alice and Jane Kean as Trixie, continued on the Gleason show for the next four years, earning Carney his fourth and fifth Emmys.

Carney credited his return to television in the 1960s with saving his life. "I had some rough times when my marriage broke up, and I was in hospitals, and the booze and the pills," confessed Art. "But there was Gleason when I needed him most. With Gleason came good times. We quarreled only once in the 20 years we worked together. The chemistry between us was right. He's Irish. I'm Irish. He's the greatest guy in the world. We'd see the show together, and Jackie laughed harder at me than he did at himself.

"Before I started doing Norton, I always was very shy. The character changed me. Everybody liked him. But unless I commit suicide, I'll never get rid of Ed Norton. You don't shake a character like that, ever."

The Honeymooners is now enjoying a resurgence in reruns and specials. The humor sprang from the love and natural relationships that were the focus of the show. And the laughter came from a live audience. As Audrey Meadows said, "We got laughs the old-fashioned way—we earned them."

Gleason credited much of the show's success to Carney. "We enjoy working together so much. I love his every move and nuance. We were as amazed and amused as the audience was at his work. We always got it on the first take." When a scene ended, the director often kept the cameras rolling to catch the ad-libs.

Commented Gleason, "That's what makes it fresh. I expect something unusual and unexpected from Art, giving me the opportunity to react. He'd kill me, and now and then, I'd get one in on him. We did it to entertain each other, and as a result, both of us came off very well."

One of the most hilarious sketches on the show was based on a boyhood experience Carney shared with his father. "My father was a very meticulous man," recalled Art, "and whenever I asked him to sign my report card,

he was what I call 'a mover.' He would shoot his shirt cuffs, make sure the light was just right and the paper was straight, and rearrange everything on the table." So when a sketch called for Ed to sign something, Carney did it with his father's flourishes.

There were so many unforgettable sketches. Another gag was when Ralph tried to teach Ed how to play golf. "First—address the ball," said Ralph with his sarcastic ridicule. Rubbery Ed bent down, his face inches from the dimpled ball: "Hello, ball."

Gleason, Audrey Meadows, Carney and Joyce Randolph may be gone, but their comedy always will live on in my memory and that of millions of others whose two favorite television couples will now always be away on a perpetual honeymoon. ❖

Oscar winner Art Carney and Robert Hy Gorman starred in the made-for-television movie Where Pigeons Go to Die *(1990). Photo courtesy the author.*

Happy Hopalong Daze

By Donna Overmyer

Some of the happy memories of my childhood are of my dad, my sister and me listening to radio shows together. We usually listened to *Hopalong Cassidy*, *The Lone Ranger* and *The Shadow*. We would gather around the radio in the kitchen and munch on popcorn while listening to adventure after adventure and imagining that we were cowboys or superheroes. Later, we would act out our own adventures.

During the summer of 1952, we lived in Lansing, Mich. I was 7 and my sister was 6 years old. It was the year Hopalong Cassidy became our favorite hero when our parents surprised us with Hoppy gear: black jackets, black hats, black gloves, and even guns and holsters. We were ecstatic.

I put on the jacket first, and then the hat. The excitement was almost too much to handle when I strapped on the holster and jammed the guns into it. Then I pulled on the gloves, and the transformation was complete. There I stood— Hopalong Cassidy in pigtails. I don't know who my sister thought she was, but at that moment, I *was* Hopalong Cassidy.

That summer, we also acquired our first two-wheel bikes. Once we had finished falling, and collecting scrapes and bruises, we were able to stay upright and even ride a good distance. Now we weren't just cowboys; we were cowboys with *horses*. I named my bike Silver, after the Lone Ranger's horse. (I was secretly in love with the Lone Ranger, and I still believe Silver is a more appropriate name for a white horse than Topper could ever be.)

Pictured left to right are the author's sister Carole Otis, her father Roger Otis and the author.

We spent many hours playing cowboys with our outfits and bikes that summer. All too soon, however, it was over and time to go back to school. We attended Everett Elementary School, which was a mile-and-a-half walk from our home. I had to coax my sister to keep moving because she enjoyed examining stones and leaves and little things she found along the way.

Imagine my surprise when we finally got to school and my second-grade teacher turned out to be none other than Mrs. Cassidy! I was in awe. I was in the presence of someone who *knew* Hopalong Cassidy! I imagined that she saw him sometimes when he wasn't out chasing bad guys. I actually *knew* someone who *knew* him! It was almost as good as being with him myself.

As I pondered this discovery, a question began churning inside me. I knew I would have to ask it, but I was a shy little girl, and it wouldn't be easy for me. I think it was weeks before I found the courage to approach my teacher. "Hoppy"—as we who were close to him were allowed to call him—was brave, so I would be too.

One day I saw my teacher eating her lunch in the lunchroom. I watched her, hoping she wouldn't leave before I had finished my own lunch. Finally, I pushed my chair under the table and threw away my trash. Then I made my way to her table. When she looked up, I just blurted it all out: "Are you Hopalong Cassidy's wife?"

I can still see her sitting there, smiling at me.

She put her arm around me and told me what I hadn't expected to hear. She *wasn't* his wife. What a letdown!

I don't remember how I survived the rest of the day, dragging that disappointment around, but it had been exciting to think about it during the weeks when I was gathering the courage to ask.

Over the years, I've thought of that incident and wondered if my teacher had been insulted. I could have asked if she were his mother, or worse yet, his grandmother. Then again, she was probably used to children asking her about Hopalong Cassidy. I know we weren't the only family listening to his adventures on the radio back in the Good Old Days. ❖

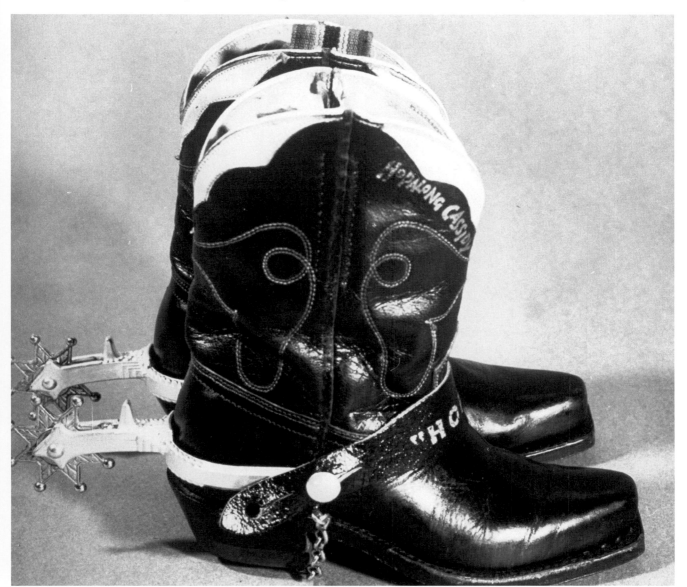

1950 Hopalong Cassidy happy boots photo by Bernard Hoffman//Time Life Pictures/Getty Images

Freddie the Fireman

By Lynne Stewart

*D*uring the days when television was our newest form of entertainment, Ron, my husband, was working as a TV newscaster. When he was offered a job as a kiddie-show host at a TV station in West Texas, the idea appealed to him. He thought it would be fun. Within a month we were on our way to the Lone Star State.

In those early days of television, the shows were not taped, but were done live. Whatever was said or done went on the air, unedited.

After making the move to the Southwest, we discovered that the shows would include an audience of 25 to 50 kids, and some of them would be interviewed on the air. Since kids tend to say whatever pops into their heads, we knew some surprises were in store, but Ron was sure he could deal with whatever might happen.

The show was called *Freddie the Fireman*, and Ron played the role of Freddie. A 1927 International fire truck, with the fire-fighting equipment removed, was used on the show, in parades and at personal appearances. The show always ended with the truck, loaded with kids, leaving the studio for a drive around the block.

> *Freddie the Fireman was a huge success—far more successful than we expected it to be.*

During the broadcast, Ron always asked some of the kids what school they attended, what grade they were in, and what they were going to be when they grew up—the usual questions that are easily answered by little ones.

Answers to "What are you going to be when you grow up?" covered everything from "a hobo" to "the president of the United States." After giving it some thought, one little boy finally shrugged, sighed deeply and said, "A man!"

When a little girl came to the show carrying a doll, Ron asked her if she was going to be a mommy someday. When she shook her head, he asked her, "Why not?"

"Cause you have to get a great big tummy first," she answered. Then, pointing off-camera at the parents' seating area, she said, "Look at my Aunt Mary's tummy—that's what happens!"

A freckle-faced little kid was asked what he had learned in school that day. He said, "A new cuss word—want to hear it?"

Another little boy announced that on the way home from school, Debbie had hit him with a book. Ron asked why she had done that.

"'Cause I shoved her," the kid answered.

"Why did you shove her?" Ron inquired.

"'Cause I want her to be my girlfriend," he said.

"Then you should be nice to her," Ron said.

Vintage fire truck photograph by Joanna Vidad courtesy www.sxc.hu

"Yeah, but I had to get her to look at me first," he explained. "There wasn't any sense in grinnin' at her unless she was lookin'."

When two little boys began giggling during a show, Ron asked them what they were laughing about. One said, "Nothin'."

But Ron kept urging them to tell him what was so funny until finally, one of the kids said, "Somebody behind us has been eatin' beans, and they did a loud poo-poo."

That was the last time Ron insisted that giggling kids tell him, on the air, why they were laughing. He learned to be very careful with his questions, but still a kid would occasionally blurt out something that would have been better left unsaid.

One little girl said her grandma had brought her to the show because her mother had to stay home and wash her daddy's underwear. "He's been wearin' the same ones for three days," she announced, "and he finally got mad."

The television station was located in the country, several miles outside the city. Built flat on the ground on a concrete slab, the building was equipped with doors wide enough to drive a car through.

One afternoon when the doors had been left open after the fire truck had been driven inside, Ron saw a rattlesnake slither into the building. With airtime 15 minutes away, only a quick search could be made for the critter, and it wasn't found.

Ron had always lived in a city. Before we moved to Texas, the only snakes he had ever seen had been behind glass in the snake house at the zoo. He was extremely upset by this unexpected turn of events.

"We can't go on the air with a snake in here," he stated. But his crew, all natives of the Southwest, accepted the situation calmly, showing a surprising lack of concern. They assured him that the snake would remain hidden. With all the noise and activity going on in the studio, it would be too frightened to leave its hiding place. If they left it alone, it would leave them alone. The children in the audience would be perfectly safe.

Unconvinced, Ron insisted that the station manager be told about the rattler. "He won't cancel the show," a crew member said. Remembering that the station manager was also a native of the Southwest, Ron realized he was beaten. With a sinking feeling, he watched as the doors were closed, trapping the snake inside.

The studio audience was ushered in and the show went on the air, but it was the worst

Freddie the Fireman show ever. Ron was a nervous wreck. As he kept watching for the snake, he was slow picking up on his cues, and he made one mistake after another.

That day, two singers known as Rocky and Cotton were appearing on the show. Ron introduced them as "Cocky and Rotten," and he wasn't aware of his mistake until Cotton drew it to his attention. "I guess the audience will decide whether or not we're cocky and rotten," Cotton said, "but our names are Rocky and Cotton."

When the show was over and the crew began to leave, Ron stopped one of the men. "Jack, that snake has to be found and gotten rid of."

"We'll leave the door open, and it'll go back out," Jack assured him.

One of *Freddie's* sponsors was a milk company, and the sponsors want to see their product consumed on television. So, with a carton of milk displayed on a table, Ron and a child from the studio audience made a game of drinking milk. At the word "Go!" shouted from off-camera, they started drinking. When "Stop!" was shouted, they put their glasses down and waited until they heard another "Go!"

It was supposed to be a contest to see who could finish the milk first. The race never lasted long because, intent on winning and being awarded a prize, the kids always drank as fast as they could—and of course, they were always allowed to win.

One night, the refrigerator in the studio was accidentally disconnected, and by showtime the next day, the milk was sour. Expecting his guest, an 8-year-old girl, to refuse the milk, Ron was afraid she would take a sip and say it tasted bad.

Forced to make a quick decision, he decided to let his glass slip out of his hand, pretend it was an accident, and in the confusion, skip the milk contest, give the girl a prize and go on to the next segment of the show. But while he was getting into position so he could drop the glass without spilling sour milk on himself, "Go!" was shouted, and the race was on.

His little guest began gulping milk, and when "Stop!" was yelled, she kept on drinking until her glass was empty. Then, with a surprised look, she put the glass on the table, said, "That was nasty!" and immediately upchucked the milk. That day the sponsor was unhappy.

In one segment of the show, Ron drew pictures of a dalmatian called Smokey. For each show, I wrote a little story about Smokey's daily adventure, and while Ron drew the picture, the story was read from the announcer's booth. When a dalmatian was left at the animal shelter, we adopted him with the idea of putting him in the show. We all loved animals, so we were delighted to have him join our family. The dalmatian answered to Charley, but on television he would be called Smokey.

For a week, Ron promised the kids that Smokey would be there in person, any day now. After he thought he had whipped up enough enthusiasm and anticipation, he had me bring Charley to the studio. I took our children, Cristi and Rex, to the show that day so they could see Charley make his TV debut.

Arriving a few minutes before airtime, I waited with Charley off-camera and out of sight. Cristi and Rex joined the studio audience. A few minutes into the show, Ron planned to say, "Well, look who just arrived!" That was my cue to unhook the dog's leash and let him go.

At home, Charley was housebroken and well-mannered, but while we waited, I discovered to my horror that he was not "studio broken." Then I heard the cue, "Well, look who just arrived!" and I turned the dog loose.

During the next commercial break, Charley was banished from the studio—but by the time he was removed, he had left his mark on both cameras, every piece of furniture on the set, Ron's easel and all four fire-truck tires. After that, Charley appeared in parades, riding in the truck, but he never appeared on the show again.

Freddie the Fireman was almost an overnight success—far more successful than we expected it to be. Very quickly it became the top-rated show in its time slot. Reservations for seats in the studio audience had to be made several months in advance.

Things were less complicated then—kids were more easily entertained. Today the show would probably only appeal to very young children, but back then, *Freddie* appealed to 13- and 14-year-old kids as well as preschoolers.

After hosting the show for about three years, Ron went back to newscasting, and *Freddie the Fireman* became only a fond memory. ❖